DETAILING
SCALE
MODEL
AIRCRAFT

from the publishers of
FineScale MODELER
MAGAZINE

DETAILING SCALE MODEL AIRCRAFT

by Mike Ashey

KALMBACH BOOKS

For my parents, Joseph and Marie Ashey,
and my sons, Thomas and Gregory.

ACKNOWLEDGEMENTS

Many people helped me over the years and in many ways, directly and indirectly, contributed to this book. Special thanks are due to Dr. Mia Anderson of Bergen Community College, Paramus, New Jersey, for awakening within me the gift of writing; Dr. Ray McAllister for his mentoring over the years; the Hobby Caboose of Tallahassee, Florida, and the Big Bend Scale Modelers Club for giving me a forum to present my modeling ideas, techniques, and achievements; Glenn Johnson of Tallahassee, Florida, for his photography and patience; Scott Weller and Richard Boutin Sr. of Tallahassee, Florida, and Major Billy Crisler, USAF, for allowing me to include some of their models in this book; Joel and Marian Swanson for their encouragement; and most importantly, to my wife, Kelly, who is my chief editor and supporter.

All black and white photos are by the author. All color photos are by Glenn Johnson/ Glenn Johnson Photoillustration of Tallahassee, Florida, unless otherwise noted.

FRONT COVER PICTURES

Top: Douglas EB-66E, manufactured by Testor, Inc.; 1/72 scale kit built by Major Billy Crisler, USAF. Center: DH-82 A/C Tigermoth, manufactured by Matchbox, Inc.; 1/32 scale kit built by Mike Ashey. Bottom: EA-6B Prowler, manufactured by Monogram, Inc.; 1/48 scale kit built by Scott Weller.

Library of Congress Cataloging-in-Publication Data

Ashey, Mike.
    Detailing scale model aircraft / by Mike Ashey.
    p. cm. – (Scale modeling handbook ; no. 18)
    "From the publisher of FineScale modeler magazine."
    Includes index.
    ISBN 0-89024-205-4

    1. Airplanes–Models. 2. Airplanes–Models–Finishing. I. Title. II. Title: FineScale modeler. III. Series.

TL770.A84 1994   629.133'134'028
                                 QBI94-1019

Contents

FOREWORD

I have often wondered what makes this hobby so special to me. I guess that, above all other reasons, it helps me to connect with my childhood and the many things that were so special about being a kid. It all started when my Dad took me along for a ride one warm summer day in 1964 and we visited a place called Vince's Hobby store in Clifton, New Jersey. I will never forget the impression it left on me. The store was a wonderland of electric trains, gas-powered airplanes that hung from the ceiling and were almost as big as I was, and walls lined with plastic models of every type. On that special day we bought a ship model, which we built and floated in the tiny pool my Dad had set up for my brothers and me. I cannot remember how many times I broke and repaired that model, but it kept me occupied and it made me hunger for more models.

Some time after my first model, I discovered that the local hardware and repair store, which was within biking distance, carried model airplanes. Within a year or two the ceiling of my room was cluttered with Aurora, Revell, Hawk, and Monogram kits of every type. I spent every dime of my paper route money on models and long hours in the basement building them. I can vividly remember those warm summer days as I rode my bike to the store while I fantasized about what it must be like to actually fly the airplane I had picked out the previous week to buy. My dreams were always filled with fighter pilot Mike Ashey's courageous exploits.

As I look back on those years, I have come to understand that building all those models served many purposes, besides keeping me out of trouble. Building models gave me an outlet to express my fledgling creativity, which has developed to the point that now I can look at a plain, basic, stripped-down model and picture it as a finely-detailed model simply by changing the picture of it in my head. It honed my skills at following instructions to assemble things, which translated to following machinery diagrams and blueprints in my later years. It allowed me to become adept at discerning spatial relationships of equipment, buildings, and site plans, which comes in handy as a practicing field engineer. It developed my commonsense problem-solving skills and instilled in me a sense of symmetry and organization. All of these attributes that I now have and which serve me well in life I can attribute in some measure to quite a few ninety-eight-cent models and five-cent tubes of Testor's glue.

Although the model industry is better now than it has ever been before, something has been lost. Amongst all the fancy high-tech kits, resin accessories, and photoetched parts we have lost the true sense and pleasure of the hobby. Many models are expensive almost to the point of being absurd, and many after-market products cost as much or more than the kits themselves. With all the hype about the recessed panel lines of this model or the highly detailed wheel wells of that model we have forgotten about the kid on the bike who yearns to expand his or her creativity and let his or her imagination run wild. We are in the process of losing an entire generation of modelers because the majority of the industry is focusing on adults instead of seeking a balance. The future generation of our hobby is growing up on electronic games, and most of them will never experience all the positive attributes that this hobby has instilled in us adults. As a result, they may never benefit from all the by-products that model building can bestow upon a young mind and propel a young man or woman to success. If we do not address this problem, at some point in the near future a vacuum will be created in the industry because their customer base is going to suddenly shrink and our hobby will suffer.

I cannot say enough good things about those manufacturers who strive to seek a balance between all age groups and offer low-cost models to our kids. I wrote this book in an effort to reintroduce to the modeling community the art of creativity, imagination, and ideas and to remind all of us that there is life beyond the high-priced, high-tech kit and that to invest in the kid on the bicycle is the best investment we can make.

CHAPTER ONE

GENERAL TIPS & TECHNIQUES

A-1H Skyraider manufactured by Monogram, Inc. (1/48 scale kit built by Major Billy Crisler, USAF.)

Over the years I have discovered and rediscovered techniques for working with plastics that have greatly advanced my modeling skills. I have condensed and refined them so that anyone can use them with success. The topics in this chapter are cataloged and grouped so you can find a specific technique easily. All the procedures and methods presented have been tested and proven in building the models pictured in this book.

REQUIRED TOOLS & EQUIPMENT

Listed below are the tools and equipment you will need to detail your model. All the items listed are mentioned throughout the book; where appropriate I have included suppliers or recommended manufacturers.

The fillers and glues I use include Testor's modeling putty, Squadron Shop's Green Stuff, the white and blue tube super glues marketed by the Duro Corporation, Two Part epoxy adhesive, marketed by the Devcon Corporation, and Elmer's or Kristal Kleer's white glue. Duro's super glue and Devcon's two-part epoxy can be found in just about any hardware store. To apply Duro's white tube super glue I use a .5mm mechanical pencil or thin wires for precise application. You also need a super glue accelerator; I have found that a two-ounce bottle will last a long time. Duro's blue tube super glue is called quick gel and is an excellent filler.

For sanding I use sandpaper from the Testor Corporation or K & S Engineering Company. It comes on a waterproof backing and can be used wet or dry. It can be cleaned with soap, water, and a brush and be reused. The grades range from 150 to 600 grit. They come in 3 x 4-inch sheets and are color-coded for easy identification. Flex-I-Files and Flex-Pad files are also handy sanding implements. The Flex-I-File works great to form and shape curves.

For sanding blocks I use small pieces of pine, balsa wood, plastic stock, or even the handles of my files. Balsa wood is especially useful because it conforms to compound areas such as wing and fuselage connection points.

For polishing I use plastic polish from the Bare Metal Foil Company or Brasso metal polish. To polish the areas that are sanded, use a cotton

7

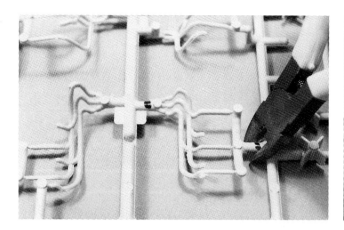

Use a pair of wire cutters to cut the trees that are connected to the parts. It sometimes helps to mark the locations.

Scribing panel lines and connecting them to raised lines is easy to do with labeling tape as a guide and a sharp sewing needle.

cloth and either of the two recommended polishes. You can't do without an X-Acto knife and numerous blades. I always keep a supply of #11 and #16 X-Acto blades, as I use them more than any other size. You will also need a small pair of wire cutters to remove parts from their trees.

For masking I recommend Scotch 3M painter's masking tape. This is the best product I have found for masking. It also makes great seat belts.

Plan on using several boxes of facial tissue per model. Tissue makes an excellent stuffer in areas that are deep and need to be masked, like cockpits and wheel wells.

You will need a glass plate for cutting decals, photoetched parts, and placards. Tape the edges with duct tape to keep from getting cut. The tape also acts as a cushion between the glass and your workbench.

For scribing I recommend plastic scribers from the Bare Metal Foil Company or Micro Mark. Both remove the plastic instead of pushing it aside, as needles do. You can also use a sewing needle in a pin vise (called a scribing needle), which works well around sharp corners. Both these tools are also used to remove control surfaces and other parts.

You will need templates to scribe circles and other small shapes. For long lines, use labeling tape for Dymo label machines.

To clean out sanding dust from scribed lines use a soft toothbrush.

To detect flaws on plastic surfaces, joints, and seam lines, use silver paint applied with a soft brush.

To clean plastic prior to applying a primer coat use Polly-S plastic prep. It can also be used between coats to remove dust and skin oils. Polly-S also makes an excellent decal and paint remover for painting disasters.

Waldron Products sells a standard-size punch set for their instruments. You will find a thousand and one uses for it besides making instrument consoles. It is a valuable tool for scratchbuilding and simplifies many projects. Waldron also markets fine console instruments and placards.

Model Technologies and others produce photoetched seat belt hardware and mesh screening with many uses. Recently, manufacturers have been supplying photoetched seatbelts complete with buckles and adjusting hardware as part of the belt. While these are easier and quicker to use, you will never be able to achieve the effect of a multiple-part seat belt, and it is difficult to paint the metal hardware. I recommend getting separate hardware for seat belts.

Evergreen Scale Model Products markets the widest selection of plastic sheet stock, strips, and rod sizes. Their plastic is easy to use, soft, responds well to sanding and shaping, and accepts paint well.

You will need a good selection of drafting templates. At a minimum you should have circles, squares, rectangles, and ellipses, and a set of small clear drafting triangles.

Round toothpicks and cotton swabs are valuable items to have on hand. Toothpicks make good applicators for white glue and for picking up

Waldron's instruments. Use cotton swabs to smooth out white glue and to clean and shape two-part epoxy.

For proper decal application you will need clear gloss and flat finishes. Testor's and Polly-S clear finish products will give you excellent results.

You will need a good supply of tweezers and micro files in various sizes. Micro Mark carries a full line of files and tweezer sets.

For airbrushing I use Badger airbrushes. I like single-action brushes because my hands are not that steady, and I find it difficult to keep the button in place as I airbrush. Clean your brush after each session and let the parts soak in a jar of mineral spirits. I also recommend investing in a compressor, even if it is a small one. Having a reliable air source is important in airbrushing. Buy a spray booth or use a large cardboard box with the top and front cut out. Moving boxes are sturdy, come in various sizes, and are readily available.

For great-looking decals you will need a decal-setting solution, but be sure the solution is compatible with your decals. I use the Microscale system, and it has never failed me.

For weathering use Polly-S weathering paints. Another good tool for weathering is pastel pencils. I run them across a piece of sandpaper and apply the residue with a soft, flat brush. I also recommend a good supply of quality flat and round brushes, especially small detail brushes.

You will need a variable-speed motor tool, a motor tool drill press, and a motor tool vise. Cutters in vari-

To cut straight strips of masking tape use a straight edge and a sharp blade. The sharp blade will insure that the masking tape will not have any feathered edges.

Sanding the gluing surfaces of small parts on a flat surface greatly improves the fit and it reduces the amount of seam work you have to do.

ous sizes, drill bits from ¼ inch down to a number 80 bit, and circular saw blades are also a must. Larger size drill bit sets can be found in hardware stores, and micro bits from number 60 to 80 can be purchased from Micro Mark in sets. You will also need a drill bit gauge and a pin vise for small jobs. I also recommend a motor tool chuck, which can also be purchased from Micro Mark. Last but not least, you should have a pair of safety glasses to protect your eyes whenever you do any cutting or drilling.

You will need razor saws of various sizes, a jeweler's saw, and an X-Acto miter box for cutting plastic stock. Blades for jeweler's saws come in various sizes.

A good supply of wood dowels in various sizes for sanding and shaping plastic is a must. A bag can be found at any crafts store. You can also get modeling clay from these stores, which is great for adding weight to the nose area of a model.

To flatten tires I use an old iron. To protect the surface and the plastic I place a small piece of waxed paper on the iron's surface when I am ready to work.

For measuring interior areas and to transfer measurements, get a good pair of drafting dividers. You will also need a contour gauge for making interior fuselage and wing bulkheads. Contour gauges can be purchased from Micro Mark along with scale rulers for 1/32, 1/48, and 1/72 scale scratchbuilding.

For mixing thinner with paint, invest in eyedroppers. They reduce the mess associated with mixing paint and save cleanup time.

For removing control surfaces and adding interior strength to wings, I use two-part resin. This stuff is great for casting parts and adding strength to control surfaces that have been cut out. It also adds a good weight to these parts and makes them easier to work with.

You will need stiff piano wire, thin spool wire, thin electronics solder, and stranded electronics wire for rigging biplanes and adding wiring and control cable detail. As you build models you should save lengths of plastic sprue in different colors, including clear. When stretched, colored plastic makes excellent rigging and colored wiring for cockpits and engines. To stretch the plastic you will need a candle and some stick matches. Small Parts Inc. of Miami Lakes, Florida, carries countless items you will find many uses for, including stiff stainless steel wire.

To transfer shapes from a cross-section of a wing or fuselage to sheet stock, you will need a grease pencil. Finally, for any detail work you will need good lighting. I use two adjustable arm desk lamps.

USING PUTTY & SANDPAPER & DETECTING FLAWS

Squeeze a small amount of putty onto a piece of paper. Allow it to flow from the tube while retaining its round shape, and squeeze out a line ¼ to ½ inch (6.4 to 12.7mm) long. For most putty applications use either a #18 flat ended X-Acto blade or a #16 angled X-Acto blade, and slice off small amounts with the edge of the blade. This will give you greater control.

Use the minimum amount of putty to do the job. Too much increases your sanding work and your chances of marring surrounding detail. When applying putty, be sure the plastic halves are well secured with glue. Any flexing of the halves during curing or sanding and scraping will cause the filler (putty) to crack and detach from the plastic.

Mask around the area to be puttied before applying it so that when the tape is removed the only putty that remains is along the seam line. This guarantees that the putty will only touch the plastic where you want it. Tape along both sides as close to the seam as possible. This will give you a thin putty line and reduce your work and the amount of detail removed during sanding.

Work in sections no more than two to three inches long and don't worry about getting putty on the masking tape. Quickly apply putty and remove the tape by pulling it back over itself and away from the putty. It is important to remove the tape while the putty is still moist, although you will need to let it dry before you sand. While this is a slow process, the thin putty line is well worth the effort and time. Before sanding, mask those areas around the putty line again to save surrounding detail.

When using sandpaper, be very careful of surrounding detail. On wings this is usually not a problem

because they are normally mated along the curved edges, making them easy to scrape and sand. Locations that are flat, have large circumferences, or are rounded, such as fuselages, require additional care. Mask as close as possible to the seam. The sandpaper will have a tendency to abrade the tape, so you might have to replace the masking tape more than once.

When you plan your sanding, be aware that the rougher the grade you use, the more work will be required to smooth the surface. To detect flaws in seam work or surface repairs, paint the area with Testor's silver paint. The silver highlights fine seam lines, scratches, bumps, and tiny bubble holes in putty. You will have to remove the silver paint before you apply any more putty, because putty will not stick to the paint.

When all the areas you sanded are flawless, remove the silver paint. The primer coat will not adhere well to the silver. In addition, the areas that are silver will have a deeper color when painted, and the finished appearance will be uneven.

The primer coat will also detect flaws. This is your last chance to repair problems before the finish coats. If you try to repair flaws after you finish painting, your chances of blending in the surface paint are not good, so do the hard work up front.

After you have finished repairing problems detected by the primer, sand the primer coat surrounding the problem areas with 600 grit sandpaper, so that it will blend into the plastic surface. Next, clean the entire model with Polly-S plastic prep. This step will remove plastic residue and skin oils, Finally, spray the primer on

areas that were repaired. If you did a good job smoothing and cleaning you will not be able to detect where you repaired.

REMOVING SEAMS

For gluing and for most seam work use Duro's white and blue tube super glues. Super glue doubles as seam filler and can be sanded and scraped like plastic. After painting, you can't detect the difference between the glue and real plastic.

Never snap a part off the tree—this may leave an indentation where the part was connected. It will almost always occur along a gluing surface, so be careful. Cut the tabs that connect the parts to the tree with small wire cutters, being sure to leave a small amount of the tab on the part. It's easier to remove the excess tab after the part has been removed from the tree.

After removing all the necessary parts, lay them flat. Carefully cut remaining tabs and clean the parts of excess plastic or flash. A #11 or #16 X-Acto blade works best for this. Be careful not to mar the plastic parts or remove any raised detail when removing flash.

Now check the fit of the two halves. Tape the halves together to ensure that corresponding aligning

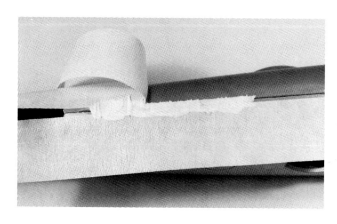

Working small sections at a time lets you remove masking tape while the putty is still wet, but be sure to pull the tape back over itself and away from the putty.

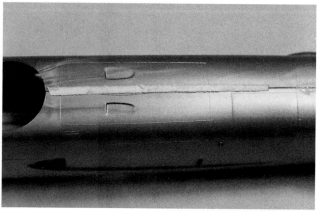

The finished putty line is very small and will decrease the sanding you'll have to do. This also limits detail loss.

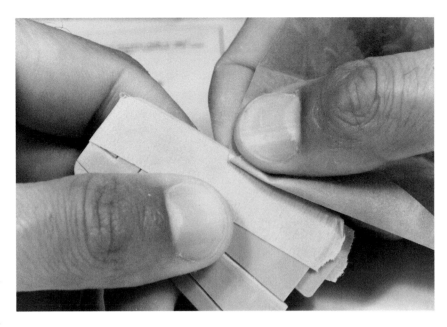

Masking tape placed close to the leading edges of a wing surface isolates the loss of detail.

pins and holes line up correctly. Check the fit in the same way on fuselages as well as on wings and tail surfaces before working on these parts.

Check the mating surfaces of both halves for flatness. Sometimes there are mold lines or bumps on these surfaces. If they are not removed, the halves will not sit flush against each other. The easiest way to remove these ridges is to scrape them flat with a #11 X-Acto blade.

As you tape, identify areas that need work and check contours and details that are formed when the parts are glued. Panel lines and hatches that cross seam lines must be lined up correctly. Take care to align corners and edges properly, or you will be doing a lot of scraping and sanding.

When you are ready to begin gluing, tape the parts together with masking tape. Use as much tape as necessary to hold them the way you want. Use super glue and a .5mm lead pencil as an applicator.

Make a small puddle of super glue on a piece of paper. When you put the glue on the paper for the first time, the paper will absorb most of it. Let the puddle dry and put more glue on top. Dip the tip of the lead pencil into the glue and run it along the seam line and between the masking tape

locations. Do not let the tip of the pencil get any closer to the tape than about $\frac{1}{16}$ to $\frac{1}{8}$ inch (1.6 to 3.2 mm). This will prevent gluing the tape to the plastic. The pencil will carry enough super glue to go about $\frac{1}{4}$ to $\frac{1}{2}$ inch (6.4 to 12.7 mm) along a seam line.

Capillary action will pull the super glue between the parts along their gluing surfaces. The glue will also act as a filler. You may need to apply several layers to cover the surface of the seam. After it has dried—about five minutes—remove the tape and glue those areas where the tape was located. Small amounts of glue work better than large amounts.

To remove excess glue and to contour and smooth the glued surfaces, scrape with a #11 X-Acto blade. Mask along the edges of the seam and sand along the seam line. Super glue is clear and, because the amount of glue is so small and narrow, it will almost appear as if there is none at all.

EJECTION MARKS

Ejection marks can either be indented or raised. They are almost always round, and are usually located in places that are hard to get at. Hasegawa's 1/32 scale F6F Hellcat is a good example. The kit has both raised and indented ejection marks on the

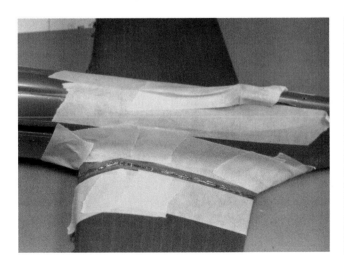

I saved much of the surface detail while filling and sanding the 1/8 inch wing-to-fuselage gap on Revell's 1/32 scale P-40 by using masking tape.

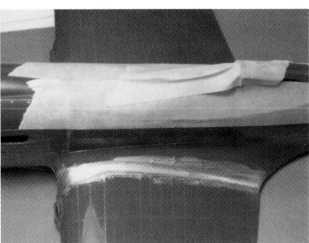

No seam correction job of this magnitude would be complete without applying silver paint to detect cracks or areas where additional gap filler is needed.

Revell's 1/32 scale Corsair got a trial fit using masking tape. This helped identify fit problems long before assembly of the major components.

to deal with because you are removing plastic instead of filling in. The easiest method is to scrape it flat with a #11 or #16 X-Acto blade and sand the surface smooth, or just use the sandpaper. For dimples, apply a drop of Duro's quick gel super glue (blue tube) and sand smooth after it dries.

RESTORING PANEL LINES

Every model builder is faced with the dilemma of what to do about panel lines lost during sanding. To minimize the length of line you are going to lose, mask as much of the surrounding area as possible. If the surface has indented panel lines, you can replace them by simply rescribing them. Be sure to scribe the new line to the same depth and thickness as those you are going to connect to.

Replacing raised lines. If the surface has raised panel lines, you can either replace the raised line or scribe the area that was lost. If you choose to replace the raised line, use a piece of stretched plastic sprue of the same thickness as the raised detail. This is tough to judge, but if you use a thin section of stretched sprue you will get pretty close. Use an oversized length, so that you can hold both ends without getting your fingers in the way, and run the sprue through a puddle of super glue. The sprue should have a thin coating of it, characterized by very tiny balls of glue. Be sure to get rid of any large globs of glue before attaching sprue, because they will mar the surface.

insides of the landing gear wheel well covers, and along the sides of the rockets. Worst of all, each landing gear has three distinct indented ejection marks.

The first step in dealing with these marks is to see if they will be noticeable when the part is assembled. Although this takes a little time and some creativity with masking tape, the effort is well worth the time invested. If the marks are not noticeable, don't waste your time with them.

Fill ejection mark holes with quick gel super glue or putty and sand smooth. If you use putty, apply it with a flat-tipped X-Acto blade and run the blade across the ejection mark to smooth it out as if it were super glue. Another method is to use Waldron's punch set to punch out a piece of plastic filler in the correct diameter. To install the disk, place a small drop of super glue at the center of the indentation, insert the disk, and sand smooth.

Raised ejection marks are easier

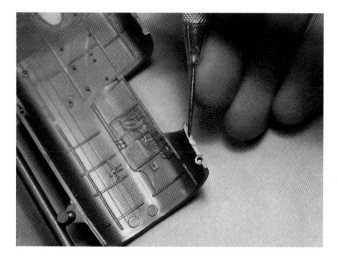

Some models have mold lines on the gluing surfaces that can easily be removed with an X-Acto blade.

The leading edges of the wings of Monogram's 1/48 scale B-29 are a tough contour area to glue: add fillers and sand. Tight masking helps align corners to reduce filling and sanding.

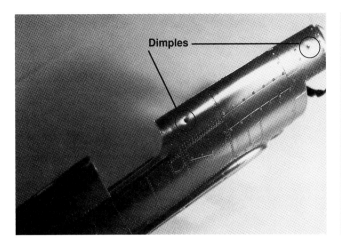

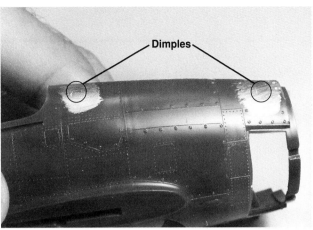

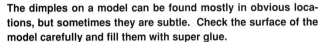

The dimples on a model can be found mostly in obvious locations, but sometimes they are subtle. Check the surface of the model carefully and fill them with super glue.

Here the first coat of silver paint has detected areas that need additional glue. Leave the paint on—it will act as an indicator of surface smoothness while you sand.

Position the sprue over the area to be replaced, holding it taut at both ends, and then lay it down. Be sure to get the ends to overlap exactly where the raised panel lines end. Do not adjust it once it comes in contact with the plastic. If you position your eyes directly over the area to be replaced you will increase your chances of doing it right the first time. If you miss, let the glue dry, sand off the sprue, and start again. The glue will begin to dry immediately once you run the sprue through it, so you have to work quickly. Once it has dried, cut the ends of the sprue so they butt up against the end of the raised line and run some 600 grit sandpaper over the repaired area to blend.

Scribing raised lines. The second approach works well on models that will have a flat paint finish. What you are really doing is playing a trick on your eyes. A scribed line will look raised because the scribe actually pushes the plastic out of the groove and up slightly on each side.

To scribe a line you will need to attach a guide to keep it straight. Use labeling tape (such as the type used in Dymo Label Machines) because it has a sticky backing and is flexible. Peel the backing off and place the edge of the sticky surface along the raised

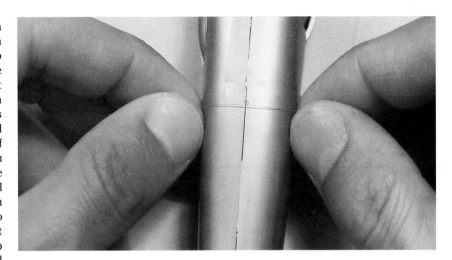

Replacing raised panel lines on Monogram's 1/48 scale B-25 with stretched sprue isn't hard, but it takes a steady hand. Be sure the entire length of the sprue has super glue on it, so that it will blend into the surface when you sand the new panel line.

The scribing technique was used on upper panel lines that cross over the fuselage on Monogram's 1/48 scale B-24J. (Model by Richard Boutin, Sr.)

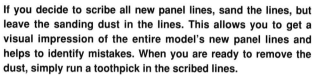

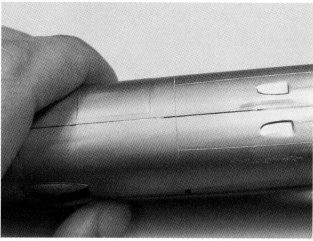

If you decide to scribe all new panel lines, sand the lines, but leave the sanding dust in the lines. This allows you to get a visual impression of the entire model's new panel lines and helps to identify mistakes. When you are ready to remove the dust, simply run a toothpick in the scribed lines.

The finished indented panel line will be difficult to detect unless your eye is almost right up to the model surface. This method is much faster than replacing the raised line with stretched sprue.

panel line. This will ensure that the scribed line will butt up against the raised line.

Don't scribe the line too deep. Two or three passes with a scribing needle will do the trick. After you finish, remove the tape and sand the area flat, but be careful not to sand off any more raised detail. Use a toothbrush with soft bristles to remove sanding dust from the scribed line.

MASKING, PAINTING & ATTACHING CLEAR PARTS

The best way to get a realistic finish is to mask the clear panels between the framing and airbrush the parts. There are two basic techniques for masking. Which one you choose depends on the framing on the part. Most framing on clear parts is raised, but some manufacturers design theirs with a high relief between the clear panels and the framing. While this sometimes appears unrealistic, when the framing is painted the high relief is hard to notice.

High-relief framing. This type of framing detail offers a quick and easy approach to masking, as long as you have a steady hand. Mask an area of the clear part so that the tape covers a clear panel and overlaps the framing. Burnish the tape down. Then take a .5mm lead pencil and follow the edge of the framing with the tip. This outlines the location where the framing meets the clear panel and provides a line for you to follow when you cut the tape. As the pencil tip pushes the tape up against the edge of the framing, the tape stretches slightly.

After outlining a section, run a #11 X-Acto blade along the edge of the framing by following the pencil line. Because of the high relief of the framing, the edge of the knife will follow the framing easily. Cut through the

(Above) The exterior of Revell's 1/32 scale P-40 windshield is finished and ready for the last step, which is to mask the inside area.

(Left) Use the pronounced edge of the framing as a guide for cutting, and be sure to use a sharp blade.

entire section of tape, so that when you remove the excess you will not peel off the tape covering the clear panel. You will notice that the tape sits up against the base of the framing where it meets the clear panel. This allows you to paint the sides of the framing, which would be impossible to do if you were painting it by hand. Once you have outlined the entire clear part, run the pencil along the edges of the tape one last time, ensuring that all edges are seated properly.

Low-relief framing. The second technique is used for clear parts without high-relief framing detail, or for clear parts that have already been installed. Cover the clear panels with small pieces of precut masking tape. Lay one strip of tape on your workbench and another right over the first one. This top layer will be used as masking for the clear parts. Next, cut long thin strips, using a small triangle as a cutting guide to ensure that the lengths of tape have straight edges. For covering small areas or when running the masking around curved framing, cut the strips approximately 1/16 inch (1.6mm) wide. Next, use your triangle to cut the tape perpendicular to the long cuts, making each cut about 1/16 to 1/8 inch (1.6 to 3.2mm) apart. Cut various lengths, so you can use the small ones to run along framing and the larger ones to cover the large areas outlined by the tape located along the framing.

When you are ready to start masking, peel up a piece, using the tip of a #11 X-Acto blade. Be sure you are not lifting both layers of tape. Start anywhere along the framing edge and work your way around the entire clear panel. As you work along a framing edge, overlap the sections of tape. Press it down with a round toothpick. Once you have completed outlining a frame, you can mask the center area of the clear panel with the larger strips of tape. When you are finished, go back over the areas where the tape meets the framing and be sure it's pressed down by using a pencil eraser on it. When you have finished, check to be sure you do not have even a sliver of clear plastic showing.

For a fighter aircraft windshield, mask the interior of the clear part and match the framing locations. While you can get away with not painting the

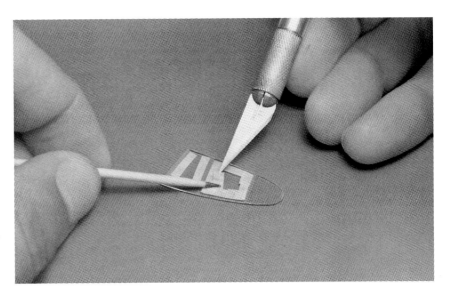

The best way to mask clear parts that don't have pronounced framing is to use small sections of masking tape with square edges.

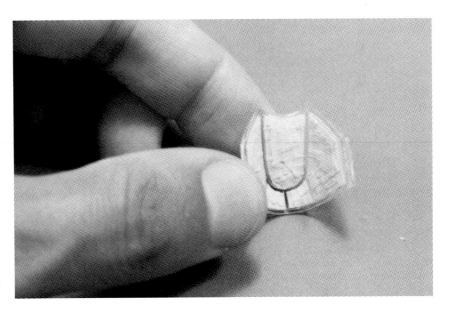

Here the inside of Revell's P-40 windshield has been masked with tiny strips of masking tape.

entire interior framing of a canopy, you can easily see the interior of a windshield, so you need to paint it. This is difficult because you don't have any raised framing to guide you as you install the tape, but you do have the outline of the tape to follow.

If you are painting the canopy, you can get away with just painting the interior framing located on the front and back of the canopy. If you decide to mask and paint the interior framing, you can cut long thin strips of tape, follow the outline of the exterior

canopy, and mask the framing that goes in the same direction. Paint these areas and remove the masking tape. When the paint is dry, mask the framing that goes in the opposite direction and paint it. This method works well on surfaces with no raised detail and seldom removes paint you masked over.

Attaching clear parts. The type of aircraft and location of the clear part will dictate whether you mask the clear panels, airbrush the part and then install it, or install it, mask it, and

Another good example of Elmer's white glue being used as a filler. Monogram's old F3F has large gaps between the windshield and the fuselage that were easily filled with Elmer's glue before painting.

The fit on the windshield of Revell's P-40 is not very good, but Elmer's white glue renders it undetectable.

then airbrush it. As a general rule you should attach clear parts with Elmer's white glue because it dries clear and is water soluble. You can wipe it off the panel areas without marring the plastic. When the model has a row of clear windows that are attached, such as on Monogram's 1/48 scale DC-3, you can use Testor's glue for those sections of the clear plastic strip that can't be seen. Except for these rare instances, always use Elmer's.

To attach a clear part, squeeze a small puddle of Elmer's onto a piece of paper and use a toothpick to apply the glue. Position the part and wipe off excess glue with a damp Q-Tip. For the installation of interior clear parts such as windows, apply glue to the perimeter of the opening on the fuselage, install the window, and wipe off excess glue.

Elmer's glue also doubles as a filler; after it dries you can apply more to fill in any voids between the clear part and the fuselage. It can also be used to contour the base of the clear part to the fuselage.

GENERAL PAINTING TIPS

For a quality paint finish on models, invest in an airbrush and compressor. This will allow you to produce the effects necessary for realism and a perception of depth. With an airbrush you can create thin coats of paint that will not cover up minute detail. You can mix paint colors, produce different tones and shades of the same color, and achieve superb weathering and streaking impossible with spray cans or a paintbrush.

For the best results, use the paint manufacturer's thinner or the thinner they suggest. The same holds true for waterbase paints. If you can't find the manufacturer's waterbase thinner, I recommend Polly-S thinner.

Since paint pigments tend to settle to the bottom of the container, it's important to mix paint thoroughly before each use. Drop a few copper BBs into the paint and shake for a few minutes. I recommend copper BBs because steel will rust in waterbase paints, changing the color.

Another good practice is to clean the neck and top of the paint bottle and the inside of the bottle cover immediately after opening the paint. This will ensure a good cap seal and longer shelf life for your paints.

The easiest way to mix proportions of thinner and paint is to start off with equal volumes of each in separate jars and use an eyedropper to add small amounts of thinner to the paint. I use standard ¾-ounce airbrush jars for all my paint mixing. If I start with equal volumes of both paint and thinner, the most the paint can be thinned is 50 percent. I also mark each bottle of thinner with the color of paint that I am mixing. That way I keep track of individual paint-to-thinner ratios. Be sure the paint in the mixing jar does not fill more than half the jar, or you will not be able to get the maximum 50/50 mixture.

Add about three-quarters of the thinner and shake the contents. Test the paint with the airbrush and add additional thinner if necessary. If you are using enamel paint, warm it before use. Warm paint will flow, spray, and adhere better than cold paint. To warm it, use a coffee cup warmer plate. It warms paint up in a few minutes and is easy and safe.

When you place the paint jar on the warmer plate, be sure to loosen the cap, so that the air in the jar will not pressurize. After warming, shake it again to ensure that the hotter paint at the bottom mixes with the cooler paint at the top.

When you're finished with the paint, leave it in the airbrush jar and label it with the manufacturer's name, the paint's color name, a federal stock reference (FS) number, if applicable, and the approximate proportions of paint and thinner. I usually end up with about ten jars of thinned paint when I am finished with a model. Since these thinned paints do not have a long shelf life, I usually pour them into a large container and clean the jars and caps. When the container is full I take it to the local recycling center for disposal.

SURFACE PREPARATION

Surface preparation is important for proper adhesion between the paint's bonding agents and the surface, and for a good finish. Prior to any painting, including priming, clean the surface of manufacturer's mold release lubricants, dirt, polishing residue, and oil from your fingers.

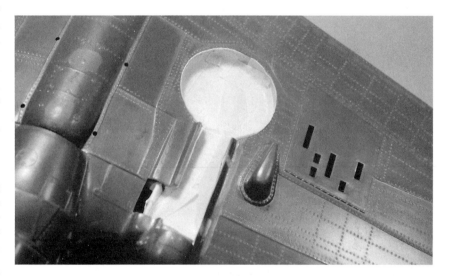

I recommend Polly-S Plastic Prep for surface preparation. It cleans plastic, leaves no residue, and makes the plastic static-free so dust won't be attracted to it. If you follow the manufacturer's directions you will get excellent results. Before painting, mask those areas that have been pre-painted or need a different color. All plastic surfaces should get a primer coat of paint prior to any finish coats (except buffable metallics).

Again, if you use a primer or some other color to check the plastic, give it an even coat before applying

For those hard-to-get-at places use tissue paper stuffed into place with a toothpick. Cover it with small pieces of masking tape for added protection.

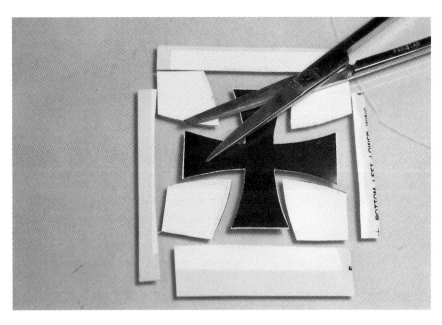

Trim as much excess clear film as possible from the decal. This reduces the chance of silvering and enhances realism.

Thanks to a good coat of clear gloss, the clear film in the center section of the Flying Tigers emblem is invisible.

cleaning time between color changes if you clean the jar and siphon and run thinner through the airbrush. Then disconnect the jar and spray to clean out the remaining thinner. Wipe the tip of the airbrush to remove paint.

After you have finished painting, take the airbrush apart and clean all the parts. I have used the same Badger 200 airbrush for over six years and it has needed repairs only once. They were free because the airbrush has a lifetime guarantee. Take care of your airbrush and it will give you excellent results.

DECALING

Cutting decals. The secret to preventing decals from getting a silvered appearance on the clear sections is to apply them to a gloss finish. If you have a flat finish, airbrush a coat of clear gloss, apply the decals, and then airbrush a coat of clear flat to restore the dull appearance of the paint. Apply the clear coats to the entire model so you won't be able to detect any differences. Just about every paint manufacturer markets clear gloss and flat finishes, and all of them work well. Another advantage to having a gloss finish is that the decals will slide easily, which is helpful when you are positioning them or if a decal folds under itself.

In most cases you can use scissors to cut out decals, but if they are close together and you have to bend the sheet to cut around a decal, use a #11 X-Acto blade and do all your knife cutting on a glass plate. Bending the sheet while the decals are dry may crack the inks.

I leave a border of approximately $\frac{3}{16}$ to $\frac{1}{8}$ inch (4.8 to 3.2 mm) around decals and cut them as I apply them. In other words, cut one decal, trim the excess clear film, apply it, and repeat the process for the next one. Nothing is more frustrating than cutting out several decals and then losing or misplacing one. This can easily happen when applying decals because the process is a bit messy. As you cut out and trim the decals, your workbench will be littered with small pieces of the decal sheet.

After rough-cutting a decal, remove as much clear film along the outer edges as possible. If the decal is a series such as "115B6" and is a small

finish paints. Without a uniform surface color, the paint finish may have a slightly different color on areas with no undercoat. Another important point in surface preparation is to make sure the plastic is the proper temperature. If the surface is cold, the paint will not adhere properly.

Use a hair dryer to warm the plastic and to get rid of any remaining dust that became attached to it while the model was in the spray booth. Hair dryers can also be used to accelerate the drying of waterbase paints, but they do not work well on oil/petroleum base paints. In any case, do not let a hair dryer get too close to the plastic; it may warp or melt it.

One final note on painting tips—clean your airbrush after each use. If you are doing a lot of painting with different colors, you can save airbrush

One of the secrets to successful decal application is to be able to hold the backing while you slide the decal into place.

decal, remove the clear film from the outer perimeter. If the series is large and the numbers or letters are spaced far enough apart, consider cutting them out separately and applying them to the model. You do not have to remove the film from central areas of numbers or letters. If you applied the clear gloss paint correctly, they will blend in.

Scissors work best for cutting long straight lines. If you are cutting along jagged edges, use a #11 X-Acto blade. When cutting small areas with the X-Acto knife you can get away with doing it freehand, but for long cuts use a straightedge to guide the blade. Sometimes when you are cutting into tight corners along a decal's edge, the cutting lines may not connect, leaving a tiny area uncut. If this happens, don't tear the carrier film from the decal—this may tear some of the inked area as you pull it.

If you are cutting large round shapes and feel confident with your scissors you can easily cut the excess carrier film by rotating the decal as you cut. Practice cutting out shapes before you actually start on the decal. Draw some shapes with a fine-point pen on thick stock paper, such as heavy bond typing paper, and practice cutting with both the scissors and the X-Acto blade. While this may sound rudimentary, I find it to be good practice, especially if I have not done any decal cutting in a while. Another approach is to make a photocopy of the decal sheet and practice on that.

The decals I find most difficult to work with are the stencils found on aircraft surfaces. They are usually small, and I recommend that you leave the carrier film on for a little extra contact surface to work with.

Small round decals are also a problem, especially those applied to fuel caps. For some reason they do not respond to setting solutions well, perhaps because their surface areas

are so small. If you punch out the clear carrier film from the center of the decal it will lie down well and mold itself onto raised detail.

Application. To apply decals, first fill a shallow tray with lukewarm water, add a few drops of Elmer's White glue, and stir the mixture until it is milky. Before picking up a decal with your tweezers, wrap the tips with small strips of masking tape to prevent damage to the decal. Keep the rest of the decal sheet away from the water to keep it dry. Dip the decal into the solution. If it is small, dip it for no more than 5 or 6 seconds. If it is large, let it sit for about 10 seconds.

When you dip, make sure the entire decal is submerged; when you

are ready to take it out, let the excess solution drip onto a tissue. Do not let the decal float in the solution, because the glue which holds it to the backing paper may dissolve quickly, resulting in the decal lifting off the paper.

After you have removed the decal from the solution, let it sit until it slides freely across its backing. While you are waiting, apply your setting solution to the model's surface. Use Q-Tips because they absorb just enough solution and won't damage decals. If you use a two-step process like the Microscale system, separate the bottles by putting them on either side of the workbench. This way you will not mix up the Q-Tips you are using as applicators.

Multiple coats of setting solution applied with a Q-Tip will draw the decal down around the smallest detail.

Setting solution did an excellent job of pulling the decal down around every rivet detail on this P-51 Mustang.

Once the decal is dry it will appear as though it was painted onto the model surface.

When you position a decal, check that it is straight, not upside down, and not reversed. Also, be careful with insignia containing a star. On fuselages, the center point of the star is always pointing up, and on wings it points toward the leading edge.

After you have applied a decal and are satisfied with it, soak up excess water and setting solution before it dries. If you let the water dry on the model, it will usually leave a stain, which can be removed by washing with a damp Q-Tip and drying with tissue paper.

To get the decal to really snuggle down around detail, apply several coats of setting solution. If it is lying against a surface with no raised detail, don't waste time applying setting solution because there is nothing for the decal to conform to. I usually apply at least three or four coats of setting solution and let each dry completely. Apply the setting solution with a Q-Tip; only wet the surface of the decal. As it dries it will pull the decal down around the detail, and it should flatten out. If tiny air bubbles appear, pop them with a pin, apply some more setting solution, and press down where the bubbles were. Each successive coat will pull the decal down around surface detail until it appears painted on. Even details like small rivets and locking screws will show, so take your time and don't skimp on coats of setting solution.

Weathering. When you have finished applying decals and the water and setting solution stains have been removed, you can apply a protective coating to them. You also need to decide if you want to weather them. If you painted the model with faded colors or if you plan to weather it, you will also need to weather the decals. Nothing looks more out of place than a weathered aircraft with bright decals. Since all military colors and painted insignia and markings lighten in the sun, use a light color to lighten the decals and blend them into the surface of the model.

The first step is to apply a coat of clear flat paint. It will provide a pro-

When the decal is ready, slide it partly off the backing so you can grasp the backing with the tweezers. Holding the backing with tweezers in one hand and a damp Q-Tip dipped in setting solution in the other, place the decal next to the surface of the model.

Lay the decal on the surface, place the Q-Tip onto the decal and pull the backing away. You can now position the decal with the Q-Tip, but don't put too much pressure on it. Once the decal is positioned, press with a damp tissue or foam sponge. Keep the decal wet while you are working with it.

If the decal is large and is a number or letter such as a "7" or an "F," be careful how you slide the backing off. These types tend to fold over or under themselves or rip. Try to move the backing away along the surface least likely to be damaged. In the case of the letter "F," move the backing to the left, and in the case of the number "7," to the right and upward. It also helps if the decal's glue is fluid and the decal is kept wet. If it does fold under itself, slide it around. Sometimes this will move the folded portion just enough to grab it with a Q-Tip and correct the problem.

Fading insignia and other markings on the fuselage sides is tricky because they don't fade as much as those on the upper wing surfaces.

A heavy dusting of dilute Polly-S dirt in combination with exhaust and gun powder stains add a dramatic effect to the underside of Revell's 1/32 scale Corsair.

tective coating and a good adhesion surface for additional paint. For weathering or fading on the upper wings or the fuselage, use Polly-S dust-colored paint from their weather colored paint series. If you do not have the Polly-S dust color, use Polly-S flat white mixed with a little Polly-S gray so the final color is an off-white.

For weathering decals on the underside of the wings and the extreme lower half of the fuselage, use the dust or flat white in combination with the dirt color if the plane operated from an airfield, and a flat gray mixed with some black for carrier-based planes. The reason for using waterbase paints is that you will be applying a large volume of thinner to the model's surface because of the paint-to-thinner ratio. The waterbase thinner will not react with paint already applied, even if it is also waterbase paint.

The fading effect on decals is subtle, so mix a dilute solution of flat white/gray or dust. Use a paint-to-thinner ratio of no more than 1 part paint to 3 parts thinner. Before you spray, test to ensure that it will not coat the model with paint. The result you want is a subtle dusting of paint particles on the surface of the model, especially on the decals. Don't get the airbrush too close to the surface while spraying. The paint should be just about dry as it touches the model.

As I said earlier, use the dust or flat white in combination with a mud color for underside weathering on planes that operated from airfields. The underside of an aircraft does not get much direct sunlight, so the fading effect will be a lot less. Insignia and markings on the lower fuselage or lower wings are usually dirt- and dust-covered instead of just faded.

CHAPTER TWO

MODIFYING COCKPITS

There are over one hundred extra parts incorporated into Revell's 1/32 scale Corsair. The combination of decals, Waldron instruments and placards, and weathering create a realistic effect.

Over the past decade the quality and quantity of detail that model manufacturers have incorporated into their kits has been impressive. Within the past few years manufacturers have been marketing high-tech kits that include photoetched parts, which add wonderful detail to cockpits, landing gear, and engines. The plastic modeling cottage industries offer a wide range of detailing accessories such as photoetched parts, metal and decal-type placards, highly detailed resin and white metal accessories, as well as superb decals. All these allow you to build models so detailed you can count the toggle switches inside the cockpit. But while they will enhance

your model, they will not take the place of scratchbuilding techniques, creativity, and imagination.

COCKPIT PAINTING & WEATHERING

Detailing cockpits means many hours of tedious work, especially in anything smaller than 1/32 scale. The number of parts and accessories you use to detail a cockpit may well exceed 100. The addition of these parts, coupled with some basic techniques for painting and weathering, will result in an accurate presentation of the real aircraft.

Adding detail, no matter how much, is a waste of time if you can't

see it. One of the tricks of master modelers is to use different shades of the same color to highlight detail and create a perception of depth. Artists use this technique when painting a picture that appears to have depth.

For example, if the interior of a cockpit is flat black and you use this color throughout, you will end up with a black hole. Creating the perception of depth is easy, but will add extra steps to your modeling approach. The end results, however, are worth the effort.

A note here on paints: although I use enamel paints for all exterior work, I use water-base paints for most interior painting. I usually end up airbrushing several shades of a color, and when using an airbrush it is much easier to clean up water-base paints than enamels. You can also accelerate the drying time of water-base paints with a hair dryer—a great advantage when time is limited.

If you are using flat black for your console, mix a few drops of flat white with it so the resulting color is a dark gray. If the radio boxes, switch banks, and flight control and engine control quadrant boxes on the sides of the cockpit are also flat black, paint a few of them the same color as the console and others a slightly lighter color made by adding more drops of flat white to the gray. If the cockpit walls and seat are interior green, make the walls a slightly darker shade of green. The sides of the seat could be one shade and the seat bottom and back and frame another. When mixing shades, keep these color differences subtle. The different shades of flat black and green will still be visible, allowing the eye to focus on detail you have added like wires, piping, seat belts, switches, and instruments.

The parts of the cockpit that are exposed to the sun should be lighter in color. In 1985, working for the Department of the Navy, I spent two months at China Lake Naval Air Station in the Mojave Desert. An aircraft boneyard at this air station had several B-29 bombers that had been there since the early '50s. I crawled through them, and among the many things I noted was that the interior green paint that was exposed to the sun was faded almost to light gray. In other areas of the plane, where the sun never touched, the same color looked almost as good as new. With this example in mind, don't be afraid to apply different shades of paint even to a single part, such as a seat.

Number the bottles containing shade mixtures and make a list of which shades you use on what parts. This way you will know which shade to use on a part if you ever need to do some touch-up. I always use light gray or white to lighten colors and never mix flat paint with gloss paint.

We have already addressed the weathering effects of sunlight, but what about wear and tear, dirt, and fluid leaks? Wear and tear on the cockpit area consists mostly of paint

The cockpit of Revell's 1/32 scale Corsair was painted several shades of interior green and flat black to create a perception of depth.

that has been worn off by rubbing, chipping, or constant contact. Seat bottoms and backs should have areas that show metal because they get worn by the pilot's back and parachute. Places where his arms rest and the area of the floorboards directly in front of the rudder pedals also get constant rubbing.

It is not always possible to highlight detail by painting parts different colors. Some examples are rivet detail, worn paint that shows bare metal, and weathering. Drybrushing can create these details. This technique uses small, flat brushes nearly void of paint. Shake a paint bottle well, then dip the tip of a dry brush into the paint left in the cap. Brush the paint onto a piece of paper, wiping each side of the brush alternately until only a hint of paint is seen.

This 1/48 scale Hasegawa Zero needs a new paint job. The worn paint effect both in the cockpit and on the aircraft's skin was achieved with a mixture of silver and black paint applied with a soft brush and a toothpick. (Model by Major Bill Crisler, USAF.)

Dust, dirt, and fluid stains are also found inside a cockpit. Adding them must be done subtly. Polly-S markets an excellent set of weathering paints that includes dust, mud, dirt, and oily black. Dust usually accumulates in cracks, corners, and crevices. Dirt is usually tracked in by the pilot or blown in when the canopy is open and the aircraft is operating from a dirt field. Dirt can accumulate behind the pilot's seat, around the headrest, on the rudder pedals, and on the floor, particularly in corners.

In older aircraft, mud is found on the floor and around the rudder pedals. Fluid stains are found on the floor, particularly near the control stick, the flap actuator, and under the rudder pedals. These types of stains are best applied with a small brush. They should look like stains or wiped-up puddles. To simulate this, place a drop of paint in an area and wipe or dab with a Q-Tip.

As you gain weathering experience, you will learn how to create a subtle effect. To avoid overdoing it, start by applying silver paint to the worn areas, then try some dust and dirt. Add fluid stains if it seems necessary. Propeller-driven aircraft, especially WWII planes, suffered a lot of wear and tear both inside and out. Jet aircraft operated from more suitable locations. Although their surfaces and exteriors can get faded and dirty, they don't suffer the same wear and tear as their piston-engine ancestors did.

Although the cockpit of Testor's 1/22 scale Douglas EB-66E has a lot of small scratchbuilt parts, all the details stand out, thanks to the various shades and colors. (Model by Major Billy Crisler, USAF.)

If you are highlighting raised surface detail, a light touch of the brush along the raised surfaces will cause tiny paint particles to cling to them. If you are adding colors to flat surfaces, you will have to press a little harder for the paint particles to adhere. Drybrushing takes some practice. It is easy to overdo it with paints, so be careful. Upon completion, add a clear coat to protect the drybrushed paint.

To represent areas where paint has worn off, mix Testor's silver with some flat black until the color is not so shiny. Drybrush with a small brush along the edges of the seat sides and the edges of panels and boxes. Use a wide flat brush to drybrush onto larger areas like the sides of the cockpit and the seat bottom and back. To represent paint that has worn off wood, drybrush the areas with a lighter shade of the paint color and then rub with 600 grit sandpaper.

MODIFYING KIT-SUPPLIED PARTS FOR INTERIOR DETAILING

Most large scale kits supply some level of interior detailing, including trim wheels, piping, throttle quadrants, and assorted electrical boxes. Sometimes these are molded into the interior siding of the model and you can enhance their appearance either by painting and drybrushing or by removing all molded interior detailing and building it from scratch. Working with the interior detailing supplied with the kit is the best starting point. While painting and drybrushing these details is adequate on 1/72 scale models, on 1/48 and 1/32 scale models the parts do not have enough depth to look realistic when

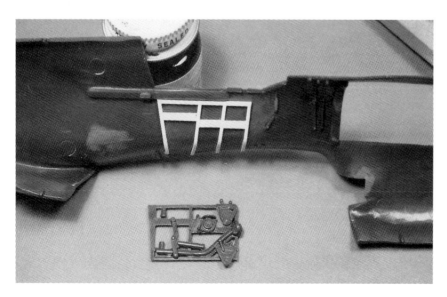

Interior framing should be as accurate as possible. Sometimes kit parts can be used as a guide.

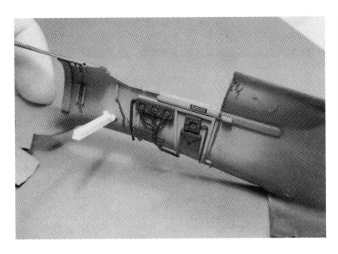

The right side of Revell's P-40 with modified electrical and radio boxes cut out from kit parts. The dial faces are Waldron instruments. The map box is scratchbuilt.

Although the sides of the cockpit look somewhat empty, once other parts such as seat, flooring, and console are added, the cockpit begins to take form.

painted. Often kit-supplied parts in 1/32 scale can be cut out, modified, or both for greater realism.

Most 1/32 scale kits, such as the Revell and Hasegawa WW II 1/32 scale fighter aircraft series, come with left and right interior sides, while the detail on most biplane models is molded into the fuselage sides. Jet fighter kits usually have a cockpit tub with the detailing added. When kits have separate interior sides, the parts they contain can be cut out, enhanced, and installed onto the inside of the fuselage. Sketch the sides of the fuselage and identify all the parts you will add. Next, temporarily install the cockpit backing, the flooring, and the console with masking tape and draw lines where these parts meet the fuselage sides. This will identify the boundaries of the cockpit sides and provide spatial orientation for the parts you plan to install. Next, draw in any interior framing your reference material identifies and install it.

Determine what is the best way to cut out the parts and assess what to do to them. Throttle quadrants can be enlarged by gluing some thin styrene stock to the back. If the control levers are not individually molded, they can be cut off and replaced with small plastic stock rod or wire. To provide a positive location for the levers, drill small holes into the quadrant, using a pin vise and a small drill bit. To reproduce the ball handles on control levers, apply a

small drop of Kristal Kleer to the tip of the lever with a toothpick.

Enhance radio boxes and other electrical boxes by adding plastic stock to the back for greater depth. If dial faces are molded into the boxes, drill them out and add Waldron instrument dials. To drill out the molded dial, indent the center with a needle held in a pin vise, drill the dial out—using a bit the same size as the punch tool required to punch out the instrument—and drill deep enough to hold the instrument. Drill a small hole in the center to allow glue to seep out the back.

Once you have drilled all the holes and test-fitted the dials, cut off all the molded switches and drill small holes in their former locations. Stretch a piece of silver or gray sprue for the switches. Install dials and switches by the same methods you used in building consoles and using Waldron placards. (See pages 35–38).

The control box for flap and trim adjustments is usually rectangular because it contains gears, pulleys, and cabling. The flap adjustment is usually a small, arm type device, while the trim adjustments are round disks. Make the flap adjustor from plastic rod or wire, and make trim wheels by punching out disks with your Waldron punch tool. On the actual aircraft, these trim wheels are usually located an inch or so above the box they are attached to. To represent this, simply punch a smaller disk size than the one that represents

the trim wheel and attach it to the back of the trim wheel disk. Some trim wheels have small spindles around their rims, and you can represent this by notching the disk with a micro file. This is a tedious process, and proper spacing of the notches is important. The best way to secure the disk while you notch it is to hold it in a small clamp.

To enhance the appearance of electrical boxes, cut off existing switches and attach new ones using the techniques described above. For indicator lights, use a round toothpick to apply a small drop of Kristal Kleer for each. Paint the appropriate color.

Almost all cockpits have piping and wiring running along the sides that either terminate at the bottom of an electrical box or run along the base of the cockpit and through the back wall into the rear of the fuselage. If you use round plastic stock for piping, place a drop of super glue at the bend locations, so that they will retain their shape. I usually cut a length of styrene rod, bend it, and form-fit it into its location.

For electrical cabling, strip the insulation off thin strand electronics wire, twist several strands together, place a drop of super glue on the twisted strand, bend into shape, and paint it. You can form-fit the wire in place once you add the parts to the cockpit sides.

When you test-fit the cockpit's backing, be sure it fits snugly between the fuselage sides. If it is too small,

The right side of Revell's P-40. The quadrants were cut from kit parts and modified, and piping and control cables were added. The wiring protruding from the back of the instruments on the console added an extra element of realism, because on the real aircraft you could see the wiring behind the console if you were looking down through the windshield.

Adding interior parts to the flooring gives an otherwise flat surface some depth. To further enhance their appearance, paint them different shades.

add thin plastic stock to fill the void. When you test-fit the interior parts, also test-fit the seat and tape it to the backing to make sure the parts don't interfere with the seat. Enhance the flooring by adding thin plastic stock to the area near the rudder pedals. This will give depth to an otherwise flat surface. You can also add piping to the floor next to the fuselage sides; run it from far under the console and through the rear cockpit wall. Once these parts are completed, paint them and glue into place.

The scratchbuilt parts installed in the Corsair's cockpit. Also visible are Waldron placards, Waldron instruments, and a variety of other scratchbuilt levers, quadrants, and switches.

Seats can be separate or molded into the cockpit backing. If the seat is a separate part, chances are its back and sides are too thick. To improve its appearance, attach sandpaper to your workbench or to a piece of wood and sand the back and sides to thin them out.

Be sure the plastic is of uniform thickness, sanding a few times in one direction and then rotate it 180 degrees, or work in a figure eight. Sides and backing should not be paper-thin—they are supposed to be armor-plated—but they should not look out of scale. Some kits come with a seat frame. Thin this as well, and remove its mold lines.

When attaching a seat, don't glue it to the cockpit backing because most seats are positioned away from the rear cockpit wall. If the kit has seat framing, the seat will automatically have some spacing. If there is none, you can attach some stock plastic to the bottom of the seat to act as a set of legs and then attach the plastic to the floor. If the seat is molded into the cockpit's rear wall, you can cut it out and work with it as a separate part.

Before you cut out the seat, make a new wall by tracing it onto plastic stock and cutting it out. Test-fit the new wall in the cockpit and make necessary adjustments with sandpaper. When you are ready to cut the seat from the cockpit wall, if there is no raised outline to work with, first draw an outline of the seat's backing. Tape the part to your workbench and use triangles and dividers to draw and measure the lengths. Be sure the lines are straight and parallel. Rough-cut it with a razor saw and sand to the correct shape and thickness. Once it has been thinned and painted it is ready for the final touch—seat belts and shoulder harnesses.

Other details attached to the cockpit backing, such as the pilot's headrest, should also be cut out, modified, and reattached to the new cockpit wall. Removing these parts,

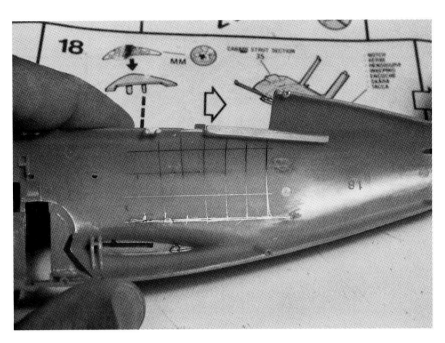

modifying, painting, and reattaching them will give the cockpit a greatly improved appearance.

SCRATCHBUILDING AN INTERIOR

Most kits have interior parts you can modify to create a more accurate interior, but some have such poor detail there is nothing you can salvage. Reference material or cockpit pictures are a must for scratchbuilding, but if you don't have any, remember that most aircraft have the same controls at the same locations. The throttle quadrant and the propeller pitch control are usually on the pilot's left. Trim selectors for the control surfaces are also usually on the left, while the flap control can be on either side. Radio boxes, electrical boxes, and switch banks are usually located on the right side, but smaller electrical boxes can be on either side. Electrical wiring and piping are located on both sides, as are oxygen bottles. Rudder pedals are located under the console, and the control column is either a stick located between the pilot's legs or a control yoke protruding from the console.

First, mark the location of the flooring, console, and rear cockpit wall on both sides of the fuselage. Some kits have no rear wall but you can make one using a contour gauge and sheet stock. The best way to secure the contour gauge is to strike a line along the interior of the fuselage where the gauge will go, tape the fuselage half to the workbench, position the gauge over the line, and push the wires until they touch the line. I always push the wires at the beginning and end of the line first because this helps maintain the position of the gauge. After you have pushed all the wires, you are ready to transfer the shape to sheet stock. I usually use

The easiest way to make interior bulkheads is to use a contour gauge. With a little practice, a gauge can save you a lot of time and frustration.

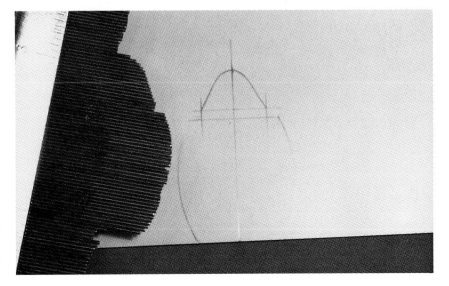

Once you are satisfied the contour gauge is set correctly, transfer the shape to sheet stock and flip it over to get the other half.

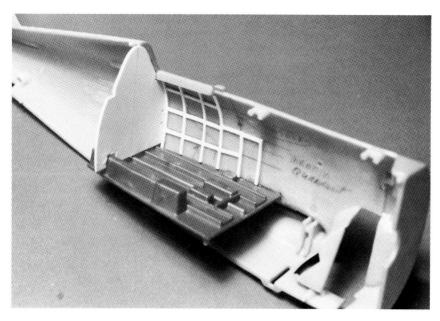

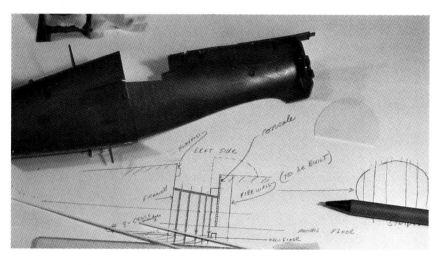

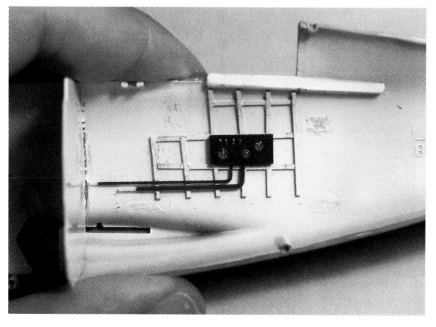

(Left) When the part you outlined with the contour gauge is cut out, you may have to do additional form-fitting to get it into place. Fill small spacing between the edges of the part and the interior wall of the fuselage with white glue.

(Center) If you are going to try a complicated project like scratchbuilding an interior, sketch where the interior parts will go and follow your plan.

.025-inch (.6mm) stock because it can be cut with a pair of scissors, yet is stiff enough to work with.

You only have half the interior contour, so strike a perpendicular line on your sheet stock and carefully position the ends of the shape on the contour gauge along the line, draw the contour, flip the gauge over, position the ends, and draw the contour again. The shape will appear jagged, but you can smooth it out by sketching the shape freehand. Now you are ready to cut it out. If you were careful to get the exact shape with the contour gauge and to transfer it precisely to the plastic sheeting, the part should fit into the fuselage. To check the fit of the new piece, tape it to one side of the fuselage and tape the fuselage together.

Framing. If you decide to install framing, remember that vertical framing is larger than horizontal framing. Use a small strip of sheet stock or a piece of scrap brass from a photo-etched set to draw lines for framing on a curved surface. If you decide to install both types of framing, do all the vertical ones first and then form-fit the horizontal ones. Since the horizontal ones will be in sections and positioned between the vertical ones, make sure they are all installed along a straight line. Install all the strips along one line, adjust them until they appear straight, and place a drop of super glue with a .5mm lead pencil on the underside of each section. The capillary action will pull the glue under the plastic strip.

Avionics boxes. To build radio boxes and electrical boxes I start with

An instrument box completed and installed, along with some electrical piping made from Evergreen plastic rod.

.06 x .25-inch (1.5 x 6.4mm) stock. If I need something thicker or wider, I simply glue more stock to the piece. Draw the shape you want on the sheet stock. Cut and shape with a razor saw and sandpaper. For instrument dials use spare instruments from Waldron's instrument sheet and add selector switches, toggle switches, piping, and electrical wiring.

Flight control trim wheels can be added using Waldron's punch set, but be sure to glue a smaller disk to the underside of the trim wheel to add depth to the part. If the trim wheel is an actual wheel instead of a selector-type dial, you have several options. For 1/48 scale kits, HO scale train brake wheels are about the right size. These parts can be found in well-stocked hobby stores. For 1/32 scale kits, buy Hasegawa's 1/32 scale Boeing F4B biplane. The kit has an excellent trim wheel which you can cast with RTV rubber. You can then make as many wheels as you need, using two-part resin.

Throttle and propeller pitch quadrants. There are two ways to make throttle and propeller pitch quadrants to give you a first-class part. The first is to take a solid piece of plastic stock, draw the quadrant's surface shape onto it, and cut and sand to the correct shape. Once the quadrant is the correct shape, place it in a vise between two pieces of balsa wood and strike lines across the top for the number of lever channels you need. Throttle quadrants usually have two or three channels, and propeller pitch quadrants usually have one or two channels. Draw the lines with a pencil, using a small, thin, flexible straightedge. Be sure they are evenly spaced. Scrap brass from a photoetched sheet works well for applications like this. Next, take a razor saw or a jeweler's saw and cut through the line into the quadrant. Be sure the cut goes a little down the side on both ends.

The second method uses a sandwich technique that requires you to draw the quadrant's outline several times. For accuracy, cut and shape one piece of stock to size to use as a master. If your quadrant has two channels you must make five drawings. I use stock of the same thickness for the front, middle, and back

panels and slightly thinner gray stock for the two inner panels.

Rough-cut the parts, but cut the top curve where the levers will be located as accurately as possible. Next, secure the back part on a piece of masking tape and position the next panel—which should be gray—slightly lower than the first. Position the next layer at the same height as the back one, add the second gray part at the same location as the first gray part and then add the final layer at the same height as the back and middle layers.

When you remove the part from the masking tape the gray sheets will extend below the base of the part. Sand the part to its correct shape using the outline on the front as a guide. To get the correct curvature on the top and bottom of the quadrant, rotate the part as you move it across the sandpaper for a smooth, curved surface.

Paint the quadrants the correct color and add levers and handles made of round plastic stock or wire by inserting the levers into the channels. The throttle handle is usually much bigger than other lever handles and is usually in the shape of a hand grip. It can be represented by round stock that is thicker than the lever arm. Other handles are usually balls, which can be made by applying a drop of Krystal Kleer to the tip of the lever arm with a toothpick. Paint the throttle handle brown, the mixture ball red, and the others black.

Cables. Cables attached to the bases of the levers, which run from

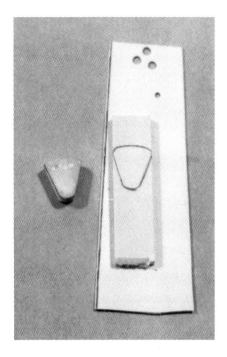

Throttle quadrants can be made from a solid piece of stock plastic that is cut and sanded to shape. Use a razor or jeweler's saw to cut the lever channels.

the side of the throttle quadrant to the engine, can be simulated with thin piano wire. Drill pilot holes into the forward side of the quadrant and run the wires through the side of the console. If you add this detail, be sure to drill the holes into the console before you glue the console into place.

Seats. Scratchbuilding seats for propeller-driven aircraft can be tedious because the parts for the seat's frame are small and the plastic sheeting you use for the seat is thin.

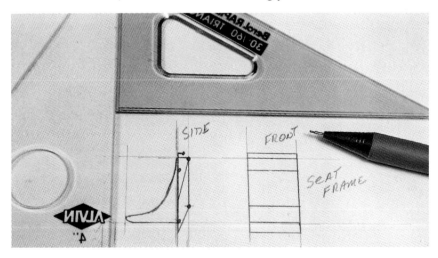

The best way to build a seat frame is to draw side and front views of the framing.

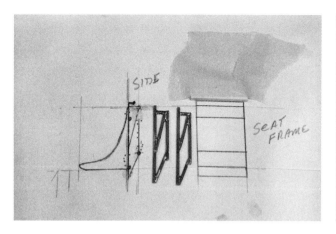

Use pins to position and hold the pieces of the frame together when gluing.

Once the sides are complete, position them on the front view drawing with pins, cut the cross members, and glue them in place.

The first step in making a seat is to build the frame.

Draw a front and side view of the frame using reference material and pictures and taking measurements of the inside area of the cockpit with a pair of dividers. When you are satisfied with the drawing, tape it to your workbench, slip a piece of balsa wood sheeting under the drawing, and begin measuring and cutting parts for the frame from either round or square plastic stock.

Some seat frames are made of tubing, while some are rectangular lengths of metal and others are a combination. For 1/32 scale kits use stock that is approximately .0375 inches (1 mm), for 1/48 scale use .035-inch (.9mm) stock, and for 1/72 scale use .025-inch (.6mm) stock. I recommend building up the sides of the frame first, using the side drawing. Then connect the sides with cross members, using the front view drawing. As you position the parts, hold them in place with pins. Be sure to locate the pins where parts will not be attached to one another. The technique of using pins to hold parts in place is the same one used to build balsa wood models, only you can't stick the pins into the parts.

Once they are positioned correctly and secured with pins, apply a tiny amount of super glue to each connection point with a small piece of wire. You only need enough glue to join the parts at the upper surface. Avoid gluing the parts to the paper. After the glue has dried, remove the pins, lift the newly constructed part from the drawing, and apply glue to the circumference of each connection point. If the part is stuck to the drawing, carefully separate the plastic from the paper with a sharp #11 X-Acto blade.

The final step is to glue the cross members to the side framing. To ensure that the side frames are vertical, pin balsa wood strips at least ¼ inch (6.4mm) thick and ½ inch (12.7mm) wide along the outer lines of the front view drawing. This will give the side framing a positive seating and ensure that they will be at 90 degrees to the cross members. If the side framing is at some other angle, the balsa wood strips are still useful; they will provide a positive seating for the base of each side frame. Set the side frames into place and use pins to hold them. Form-fit the cross members one at a time and glue, using the same thin wire. Remove the completed frame from the drawing and finish gluing the pieces.

Now you are ready to work on the seat. Since seats can be sanded down to the correct thickness by running them across stationary sandpaper, you can construct them with thicker plastic stock. This makes it easier, especially when you are working in smaller scales. Use .025-inch (.6mm) stock for seat sides and .017-inch (.4mm) or .0109-inch (.3mm) stock for the seat backing and base.

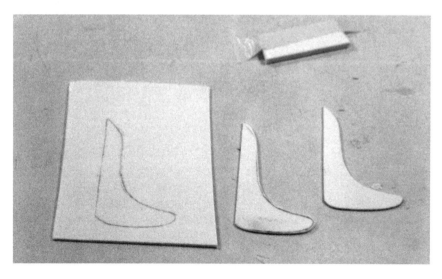

Rough-cut the seat sides, attach with white glue, and sand to the proper shape. The white glue comes off easily when you soak the part in water.

Draw the sides of the seats directly onto the .025-inch (.6mm) plastic, rough-cut the parts, and shape so they are perfectly matched. The easiest way is to glue them together with Elmer's glue and use micro files and sandpaper to give them their final shape. When you are finished, separate the parts with a #11 X-Acto blade and wash the excess white glue off with soap and water.

Now draw a front view of the seat onto the plastic stock you will use for the backing and base. The simplest seat is one that does not have a rounded bottom where the backing and base meet. For this type of seat, position the balsa strips to act as guides for the seat sides, position the sides on the drawing, and then glue them. Run a tiny bead of glue along the inner contact area between the side of the seat and the backing. When the glue is dry, remove the balsa blocks and glue a piece of sheet stock to the bottom of the sides. Cut and shape the excess plastic. I usually cut the excess with an X-Acto blade and sand the last 1/16 inch (1.6 mm) by running the seat across a stationary piece of sandpaper. This is also the best way to thin the sides if they are too thick.

If the seat has a rounded base, draw a long rectangle onto the sheeting, correctly locate and glue the sides on the upper portion of the rectangle, and use the remaining area of the rectangle as the seat's bottom. After the glue has dried, trim excess plastic, leaving a lip of 1/8 inch (3.2 mm). Slowly rotate the plastic sheeting around the back and bottom of the seat, gluing the sheeting as you work toward the forward edge of the seat.

After you have glued the bottom half in place and the glue is dry, trim the excess and sand the seat to the correct shape and thickness. I sometimes add an extra layer of plastic to the back and base for strength and sand it down. Sometimes even 1/32 inch (.8 mm) of additional plastic can add considerable strength to a thin piece. Finally, check for cracks and excess glue with silver paint. Be sure to remove this paint before priming and give the surfaces of the seat a final sanding with 600 grit sandpaper to smooth out any scratches.

Glue the sides to the backing and run a bead of super glue along the inner joint to secure the parts. If the seat has a rounded base, simply roll the sheeting around the base of the sides and glue.

Jet aircraft ejection seats are complicated pieces of machinery. Most jet aircraft kits have good seats which can be improved by adding plastic stock such as tubing, small boxes, and strips of wire. Or you can purchase an aftermarket resin ejection seat with a lot of detail added. If the seat from your kit has molded seat belts, remove them with a small piece of sandpaper wrapped around the end of a piece of balsa wood. The balsa wood should be small enough that you can sand the belt off the side or from top to bottom. If you use a fine grit, you won't mar the seat's cushion detail. Extra detail and seat belts, along with proper painting and

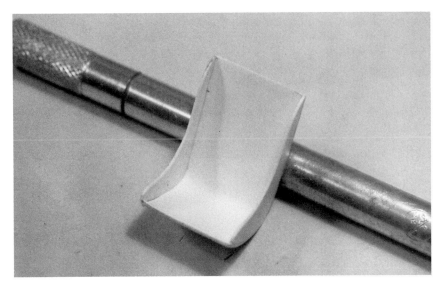

The completed seat is ready for final shaping. The corners of the seat still have to be rounded. A thicker piece of sheet stock will be added to the bottom to reinforce the base.

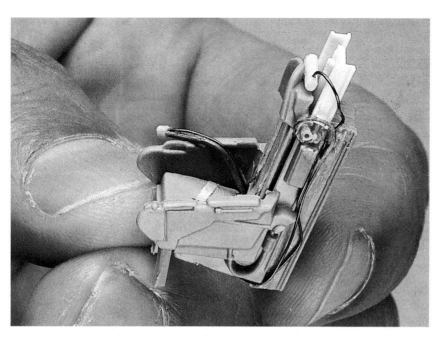

Ejection seats for jets are hard to scratchbuild, but one way to improve the appearance of kit seats is to add wiring, framing, and piping to them. This is a kit ejection seat from Monogram's 1/48 scale F-100.

drybrushing, can easily transform a kit ejection seat into a work of art.

MAKING SEAT BELTS & SHOULDER HARNESSES

Seat belt hardware adds a lot of realism to the cockpit. Model Technologies and other cottage industry manufacturers market high-quality photoetched hardware that is easy to use. Some modelers use paper to represent seat belts and shoulder harnesses, but I have found it difficult to work with. Instead, I use 3M masking tape, which does not rip easily, takes

The back side of this P-51 Mustang seat has its shoulder hardware attached. The seat belt length has been folded over the seat. The last step will be to add the buckle and length-adjusting hardware.

paint well, and looks realistic.

For 1/48 and 1/32 scale kits use two layers of tape back to back. On 1/24 scale kits use three layers, and on 1/72 scale kits use a single strip. To work with masking tape, lay it down on your workbench, draw the correct seat belt or shoulder harness width, and cut it out with a #11 X-Acto blade. Cut individual lengths longer than you need at first. Make enough for both seat belts and shoulder harnesses. Seat belts are slightly wider than shoulder harnesses, so be sure to measure and cut different widths.

For good-looking leather belts, I paint the masking tape with a base color of Polly-S earth brown and highlight it by drybrushing with Testor's wood color. When you add the wood color, you get streaks of a lighter color, which helps represent the discoloration leather undergoes when it gets dirty, wet, and exposed to the sun. To represent canvas use either a lightened olive drab or a light gray. Highlight these colors with a lighter shade of the base color and drybrush some Polly-S dirt for weathering. Definitely use the dirt color on light gray canvas, because light colors always show even the slightest dirt.

Once the paint is dry you are ready to add the hardware. For the

seat belts you should have two long lengths. The easiest way to attach the buckles correctly is to slide them onto the belt and fold a small portion of the belt under itself. Position the hardware in the crease of the fold, making sure the portion folded under is positioned exactly under the upper section, and place a tiny drop of super glue on the underside of the belt to secure the fold.

Shoulder harnesses can be two individual lengths with separate adjustments or one long length—the photoetched parts are set up for both designs. When building a seat with one continuous length, measure the approximate length you will need. Attach the necessary hardware to the back of the seat with super glue, fold the belt length in two, run it through the loop, lay it over the seat, and cut it to the appropriate length. The shoulder harnesses should be as long as the seat's back, and the tips of the harnesses should almost touch the seat bottom. Add extra length, so that it can be folded under itself. For both types of harnesses, add the mid-length strap length adjusters before adding the end buckles. Sliding these length adjusters takes a gentle touch; be careful not to bend them. Once you have them in place, add the end buckles the same way you did the seat belts.

For belt grommets, place four drops of silver paint in a box pattern on the top of each belt that needs hardware at its tip. Apply the paint with a sharp-tipped round toothpick. Don't put lot of paint on the toothpick; you are looking for a subtle effect, not four giant globs of paint.

To attach seat belts to the seat bottom, fold them over the edges of the seat and lay the remaining length across it. After you cut the belt to the correct length, place small drops of super glue on the bottom of the belt and press it onto the seat. The seat belts should be long enough to touch the opposite side of the seat. Since harnesses lie against the back of the seat, add a small drop of super glue toward the end of each harness and press it against the back of the seat.

GUNSIGHTS

Many manufacturers supply some type of gunsight part that usually has the correct shape but lacks detail. Most WWII fighter aircraft were fitted with some type of reflective gunsight centered either at the top of the console or above, while modern jets have heads-up displays that combine computer-aided gun and missile aiming along with instrument readings. The reflective glass for the gunsight is positioned so the pilot can look through the reflective glass at the target.

Adding some detail and modifying kit-supplied gunsights adds a pinch of realism to the cockpit. First, define the shape of the gunsight using sandpaper and micro files. Define edges and corners and make sure round shapes are actually round. Be sure to remove any flash, mold seams, and dimples on the surface of the part. Flash and mold seams can be removed with a #11 X-Acto blade, but dimples must be filled.

Once you have better defined the gunsight's shape, identify the locations of any clear parts like prisms or reflective glass. If there is round clear glass located on the gunsight—such as on a P-51 Mustang—match the closest diameter from Waldron's punch set, identify the drill bit size, and drill out these locations. Go only deep enough to allow a piece of clear plastic to sit either on or just below the surface. The shape of the end of the drill bit will form a ledge on the inside wall of the hole, and the clear plastic disk will sit nicely against it. Be careful when drilling, because the plastic will be thin afterward. Punch out the appropriate size disk from clear plastic stock and glue it in the hole using white glue. The easiest way to pick up the clear disk is with the end of a round toothpick moistened with saliva.

If the reflective glass is located on the gunsight, the manufacturer probably molded the correct shape and location, but molded it as part of the gunsight instead of supplying a separate piece of clear plastic. The trick is to modify the area so you can install a piece of clear plastic. Since reflective glass is located on the top of the gunsight and the sides that hold the glass in position are metal, all you have to do is cut out the center of the plastic, leaving thin walls on both sides. Use your micro files to

Some World War I aircraft used rope for a seat belt. The small section of rope was taken from Revell's 1/96 scale sailing ship model USS Constitution.

slowly remove the plastic while shaping it. Dig into the plastic with the triangular file, using the flat surface files to define the bottom and sides. Be careful as you thin out the sides—replacing a side with plastic sheeting will be difficult due to its small size. When the area is shaped, use a pair of dividers to measure where clear plastic will sit. Transfer the measurements to clear stock, cut out the part, and glue with white glue.

You can dress up the sides of the gunsight with small plastic disks punched out with Waldron's punch tool. A switch or two of stretched sprue, or a small instruction decal or scrap plate from a placard set really adds realism. Most gunsights are a light shade of flat black. Mix a small amount of flat white with your flat black. Be sure the gunsight is not the same shade as the console. You want it to stand out, and if you paint it the

Revell's stock 1/32 scale P-40 gunsight, modified to sport reflective glass and adjusting dials. The disks were punched from sheet styrene with Waldron's punch tool.

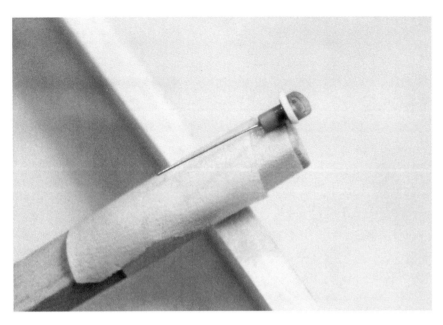

Scratchbuilt gunsights are not hard to do. This one is made from two sizes of round stock, a small piece of flat stock, and a piece of wire.

same color as the console, the detail won't be visible. Disks and switches should also be a lighter shade or a different color than the gunsight. Don't add clear parts until you have finished painting.

Remember, no one will stand over your model with reference pictures checking to see that every detail is exact. You are trying for a balance between realism, perception of depth, and overall presentation by building an interior that speaks directly to the viewer's eyes.

ADVANCED TECHNIQUES WITH WALDRON PRODUCTS

I've put these techniques for adding cockpit realism at the end of this chapter because they require some more advanced skills. Although manufacturers now supply pho-

toetched parts for consoles and cockpit placards for many aircraft, you may need or wish to build your own. With the help of some Waldron products and the following techniques, you can.

Build a console. Waldron markets flight instruments and instrument bezels that are easy to install and moderately priced. The first step in building a console with these products is to get some reference material on the aircraft, including cockpit pictures of the console. Without this material, you will have only the kit's console for a guide. Study the pictures and become familiar with the location of instruments and switches.

Next, make a sketch of the console, including the instruments, which need only be represented by circles. The exact location of each instrument on the sketch is not as important as including all of them and their approximate locations with respect to one another. Most aircraft consoles are structured so the most important instruments, such as the attitude indicator (more commonly known as the artificial horizon), the turn and bank indicator, the speed indicator, and the altitude indicator, are located toward the center.

Strike a reference line down the approximate center of the sketch. Since most instruments follow a vertical or horizontal line, several should be along the same line.

Once you have completed the sketch, label each circle with the name of an instrument and match the instrument to its location on the Waldron instrument sheet. They are numbered; the instruction sheet also has a cross index that lists each number and the type of instrument, making them easy to find. Write the Waldron instrument number next to the instrument's name on the sketch, and write the punch size you will need. Determine what size punch you need for each instrument by matching the punch head with the instruction sheet diagram. To prevent any mixups between instrument number and punch size, draw boxes or circles around the instrument numbers.

Once you have a complete drawing, decide how you want to make the console. Waldron recommends a slightly bigger console so all the

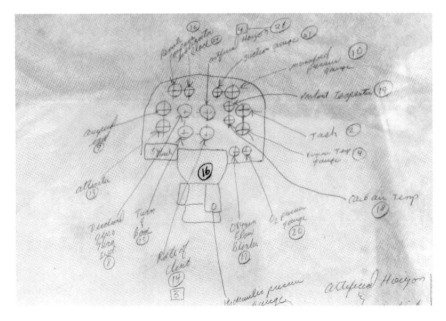

Sketching the console with all necessary information included on each instrument helps you coordinate the instruments and their locations.

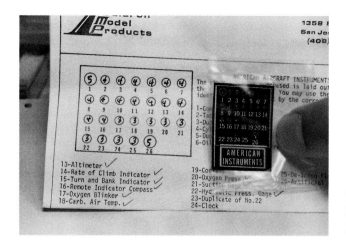

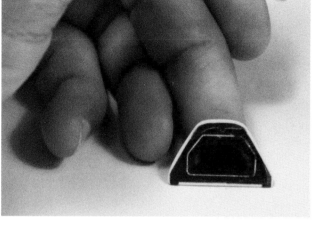

Write the correct punch size for each instrument onto the diagram. This will give you a reference sheet to check before punching an instrument.

Adding extra strip stock to the kit's console helps increase the surface area so you can fit all the instruments.

instruments will fit. This means you will have to carefully remove some interior plastic and do a lot of trial-and-error fitting. I make all my consoles using a simple sandwich construction technique that incorporates the kit's console, and I have never had a problem making the instruments fit.

First, check the fit of the kit's console inside the cockpit. Tape the fuselage halves together and insert the console. In most cases it will not fit snugly, which means you must add thin plastic strips along the sides. Adding this plastic results in a more realistic finished console with little or no spacing between the edge of the console and the cockpit wall. It also gives you extra room to play with when locating instruments. Once you have glued the extra plastic strips and checked the fit, sand the surface of the kit's console flat. It will become the back half of the new console.

Next, trace the modified kit's console onto sheet plastic no more that .015 to .017 inches (.38 to .43 mm) thick. This is the best thickness for Waldron's instruments, which are approximately .0109 inches (.3 mm) thick. Strike a straight line onto the plastic sheeting; this will be your reference line and the base line for the new console face. Carefully locate the base of the kit's console directly on top of the line at least ½ inch (12.7 mm) away from the edge of the sheeting. Trace around the edge of the console with a .5mm lead pen-

cil, then draw a box around your tracing about ½ inch (12.7 mm) away from the console's edge.

When you have finished drawing the box cut it out, tape it to your workbench, and tape the longest side of a triangle or other straightedge along the base of the console drawing. The straightedge must be directly on top of the bottom edge of the drawing, since the bottom edge serves as the base from which to draw vertical and horizontal lines for locating instruments. If you place the straightedge below the edge of the console drawing, be sure it is parallel with the bottom edge.

Locate the center of the drawing by measuring its base and dividing by two. Mark this location and strike a line from top to bottom by placing

another triangle along the base of the triangle you taped to the desk. Now you have a reference point between the sketch and the console drawing.

Start drawing vertical and horizontal lines on the console to locate instruments. It will make the job a lot easier if you start with the largest instruments. Or start with the ones in the center of the console and work toward the outer edges. Either method will reduce the likelihood that you will have to erase lines and start over. It's a slow process that requires you to continually refer to the sketch and your documentation for the locations, alignments, and groupings of instruments.

Once you have drawn some center lines, start drawing circles onto the console using a circle template.

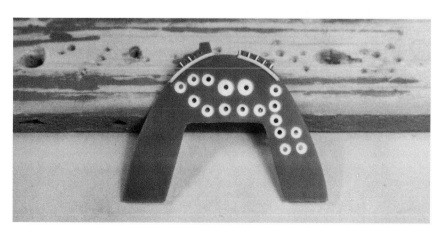

Another good example of how the kit's console can be used. Here Revell's 1/32 scale Corsair console was thinned out and then modified.

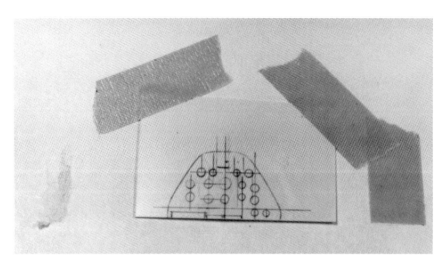

When all the instrument locations are drawn, the console face should look just like this.

Be sure the size of the circle you use corresponds to a correct punch size for an instrument. I have all my templates labeled for each punch size. I start with the largest instruments first and get their locations set; then I can use them as reference points as I add more. Getting the locations exactly correct is not as important as getting them evenly spaced and in line with one another.

If any switches are to be added, locate their positions on the console and use a small drill bit to drill pilot holes. For 1/32 scale consoles use a number 73 or 74 bit; for 1/48 scale kits use a number 78 bit; and for 1/72 scale use 78 to 82. If several switches

are in line, be sure they are evenly spaced and straight. The best way to do this is to strike a line and use a pair of dividers to space them.

When you have drawn all the circles and located all the switches, remove the new console from your workbench, cut out the outline with a pair of scissors, and slide it into the punch guide. Carefully position each circle under the correct punch hole. Be sure to pinch the console between the upper and lower parts of the punch guide so it won't slip. Centering a circle under a punch hole takes some practice. I suggest some trial runs before you do the real thing.

After you have punched out all

the instrument holes, clean the plastic burrs around each hole so your instruments will fit correctly. Take a dill bit the same size as the punch and run it through each hole with a twisting motion. To test whether any burrs remain, run a punch through. If it binds or feels tight, you need to open up the hole. If you don't have a bit of the correct size, use a #11 X-Acto blade, but be careful not to gouge the edges of the hole.

When the punches slide through their respective holes, you are ready to glue the new console to the kit's console. Position them so the edges don't overlap, and apply glue with the tip of a .5mm lead pencil on select locations around the perimeter. After it dries, run a bead around the perimeter. Don't let any glue get into the holes—it will prevent the instruments from seating correctly. I call this process the sandwich technique.

When the glue is dry, sand the edges smooth. Take a small drill bit, center it in each instrument hole, and drill through the backing. These holes will allow the white glue you will use to glue each instrument to seep out the back instead of overflowing onto the face of the instrument.

Now that the console is complete, you are ready to paint it and apply the instruments. Most consoles are flat black. Whatever color you choose, lighten it up with some white to create a perception of depth between the instruments and the face of the console.

When you are ready to apply the instruments, peel off the paper backing on the instrument sheet and paint the back of the instrument sheet flat enamel white or whatever color your reference material calls for. If you don't have any information, just use white. After the paint has dried, slip the instrument sheet into the punch guide and begin punching the instruments out. Punch one at a time and install it before doing the next one. This method is slow, but it will prevent you from losing any instruments. The sketch and reference information you added will allow you to punch an instrument, locate it on the drawing, and place it on the console.

To pick up instruments I cut the tip off a round toothpick, wet the blunted tip with my tongue, and pick

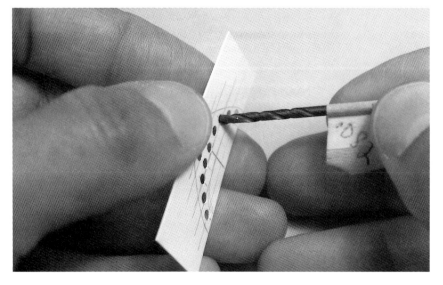

Clean the burrs from around the punched hole, so that the instrument will fit properly. If you don't have the same size drill bits, use a #11 X-Acto blade.

On small instrument consoles use Dremel's drill press to drill holes in the center of each instrument location. The holes allow glue to seep out the back.

The completed console is ready to be primed and painted. This console will be part of a Hasegawa P-51 Mustang.

up the instrument face first. Put a small drop of Elmer's white glue in the hole where the instrument will go and insert the instrument. Once it is in, it is hard to rotate, so get it right the first time. If you get it wrong, pop it out from the back and try again.

To make switches, stretch black or silver plastic sprue over a candle. Don't make it too thin. Since switches are too small to handle and hard to cut to a consistent length, take the length of stretched sprue and cut it into sections about ¼ to ½ inch (6.4 to 12.7 mm) in length. Glue them into the switch holes, using white glue. Be sure they are straight with respect to one another and the console.

After the glue has dried, lay the lengths of plastic against a sanding block and cut to length with a #11 X-Acto blade. If you lay the blade across the lengths of stretched plastic, you can cut them all at once.

Cockpit consoles sometimes have instruction cards, which can be simulated with small decals. Monogram's 1/48 scale B-29 decal sheet contains dozens of small decals that can be used for this purpose on both 1/32 scale and 1/48 scale consoles. Another source is Waldron's Placards, which can be modified to look like instruction plates.

The last step is to install instrument bezels (the grooved rims around the instrument faces that protrude from the console). This is really an option—although bezels enhance the console, you can get by without them. If you decide to add them, cut them out one at a time on a glass surface with a sharp #11 X-Acto blade. Although bezels are small, they are stronger than they look and can be handled with a pair of tweezers. Secure the bezel with a toothpick as you cut the stubs that connect it to the tree. Sometimes bezels can get launched from their trees when you cut the second stub, so hold them down carefully.

Before you attach the bezel to the console, paint the edges where you cut it from the tree. Chances are some shiny brass will be visible; this can be cured with some flat black.

Use a flat-ended, round toothpick with a moistened tip to pick and position the instruments.

The cockpit of a Corsair is filled with switch banks that can be easily reproduced with stretched sprue.

Revell's stock 1/32 scale P-40 instrument console with Waldron instruments and bezels and two additional instruction plates cut from decals. The only thing left to do is add the switches.

graphic negative slide material as the CRT display. Form-fit it into the CRT box and glue with Elmer's white glue. To distinguish the console from the CRT boxes, paint them different shades or colors.

Placards. Waldron Products also markets thin aluminum sheet cockpit placards for engine throttle quadrants, radio boxes, electrical and switch panels, gun controls, and trim and flap controls. Waldron Products also includes plastic disks and boxes for their placards. I use them in combination with both scratchbuilt and modified kit parts.

Even though Waldron includes pictures of finished kits in the assembly instructions, having pictures of the actual cockpit will help you immensely during assembly. It also helps to sketch the sides of the cockpit and draw in all the shapes to be added. This gives you spatial orientation inside the cockpit. It is important because all the parts you add must fit, and when you close the fuselage, the parts cannot interfere with other interior parts such as the seat.

Next, decide how you want to build up the cockpit. I always to use what the kit manufacturer supplies, if possible, because it saves time—so don't be afraid to modify kit parts to make them fit the Waldron placards.

Once you have become familiar with the real cockpit and identified the kit parts you want to use and those you need to make, you are ready to start cutting out placards. The secret to working with Waldron

Don't attach bezels with anything but white glue or Kristal Kleer, which will dry clear and can be removed easily with a toothpick.

When you are ready to attach a bezel, apply white glue to the back side with a toothpick as you hold it with tweezers. Carefully lay the bezel over the instrument. Avoid getting glue on the instrument face. Position the bezel, press it down, and use a sharp toothpick to adjust it and remove excess glue.

As an alternative to using Waldron instruments, console decals can be used to produce a fairly good console. Some manufacturers supply

them with some of their kits, and aftermarket suppliers such as Super Scale International include instrument decals with some of their decal sheets. On 1/72 scale kits console decals look okay, but on 1/48 scale and 1/32 scale kits the flat appearance of decals can be readily seen and detracts from the effect. To create a realistic console using these decals, use the sandwich method to make a new console. Punch out the instruments from the decal sheet and install them just like Waldron instruments.

On many modern jets individual instruments have given way to CRT displays. To make them, use photo-

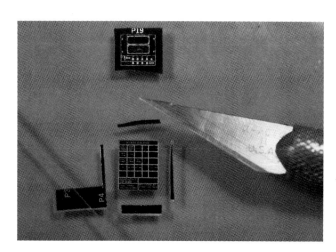

Rough-cut large placards and trim to size on a glass plate, using a straightedge.

Cut small placards by positioning the blade over the cut line and pressing down.

Using oversized stock makes mounting placards easy and ensures they will be centered on the plastic stock.

The same P-51 throttle quadrant after the plastic was trimmed and sanded. With the levers added, the part is ready to be installed.

placards (or any type of placard made from metal or plastic) is to use only a sharp #11 X-Acto blade. If you cut with scissors you will bend the edges of the placard, and flattening them out may scratch the surface detail.

Rough-cut a placard on a glass plate, leaving some sheeting around the outline. There are two ways to trim the excess. The first is to place a small straightedge along the cutting line and run the X-Acto blade along it. You may need to run the blade over the cut more than once, so don't move the straightedge until you are done. This works well for large box-type placards. For small ones, secure the placard with a Q-Tip so you don't lose it as you cut. Position a #11 X-Acto blade over the edge to be cut and press down hard. This works

well for placards with cutting edges smaller than the length of the blade.

If the placards have curved cutting lines you will need to cut around the curves by using a series of tangent cuts. Once the part is glued to its backing, you can round it off with sandpaper. If the placards are round, punch them out with Waldron's punch set, but if the size does not match a punch diameter, rough-cut the part and make tangent cuts along the edges of the circle. Here again you can round off the part after it is glued to its backing. To make sure you don't lose any parts, work with one placard at a time.

Next, bend the placard into its proper shape. Waldron's instructions explain how to bend placards and at what angles they need to be bent. If

there are multiple bends in a piece, they provide side-view drawings of the finished part for reference. Placards for square and rectangular shapes usually have only two sides, the top and the front, and these are the easiest to bend. I use combinations of plastic strip, my X-Acto blades, and edges of sanding blocks to help bend them into shape. If you make a mistake you can flatten the placard and try again, but this will usually only work once.

After you have finished bending, you are ready to attach the placard to its plastic backing. Although Waldron supplies plastic shapes for some of the smaller placards, you will have to use plastic stock for the larger ones. I use stock that is thicker and longer than necessary; then I don't have to

The left side of Hasegawa's 1/32 scale P-51 Mustang with instruction plates and some of the Waldron placards installed. The piping was made from Evergreen rod bent into shape.

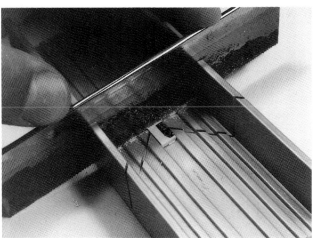

To cut down the sides of box-type placards, use a razor saw and a miter box.

It's easier to install oversized stretched sprue and cut it to size than to cut exact lengths from the start.

The switches on the Corsair cockpit panel were cut to their correct length with small wire cutters and painted silver.

worry about getting it positioned correctly. This is because the super glue will secure the placard the instant it touches the plastic. After the glue is dry, cut the stock down to within $\frac{1}{10}$ to $\frac{1}{32}$ inch (2.5 to .8 mm) of the placard. Sand the remainder off by running the plastic across stationary sandpaper.

After you have shaped the stock, paint it to match the black color of the placard. Protect the placard's face from paint with masking tape.

The last step before installation is to add selector and toggle switches. For selector switches choose the Waldron punch size that matches the dial location on the placard, punch

out a small disk, secure it on a strip of masking tape, and glue a small piece of strip stock across the center of the disk. When the glue dries cut the strip stock so its edges are even with the disk's edge. Paint the disk a slightly lighter color than the placard. When the paint is dry glue the selector switch in place. Be sure to position it correctly—the plastic strip you glued to the disk should be pointing toward an inscription on the placard.

Toggle switches can be added the same way as described in the section on consoles, but I recommend painting them a different shade of black so they stand out—or use silver or gray sprue. Drill holes through the

placard to place the switches, indenting the drill locations with a pin first so the bit will be properly positioned. The switches should be evenly spaced and in a straight line. They don't have to be all pointed in one direction (some will be off and others will be on).

If the placards have indicator lights, they can be simulated by adding a drop of Elmer's white glue or Krystal Kleer to each location using a round toothpick as an applicator. These glues have a high surface tension and will form a perfect hemispherical shape. After the glue has dried, paint it the appropriate color. If you have no information on indicator light colors, use red and green.

When you are ready to start adding the placards to the cockpit walls and flooring, first attach parts such as the cockpit rear wall, the seat, the flooring, and the console. Doing so will allow you to fit everything in place without having to worry about parts interfering with one another. Complete one side of the fuselage at a time. Close the fuselage halves frequently to check the fit of each part.

If you decide to use decal placards instead of Waldron's aluminum placards, the same construction techniques apply, but be sure the decal is properly applied and has a good protective coating. To ensure good adhesion, apply it to a gloss surface and give it several overcoats of a clear flat finish. This will allow you to drill holes in the decal for switches without ripping it, and to glue plastic stock to it. For all gluing use either Krystal Kleer or Elmer's white glue.

Form-fit each placard into place as you construct the interior. The right side of Hasegawa's P-51 is complete and ready to be mated with the other side of the fuselage.

CHAPTER THREE ENGINES

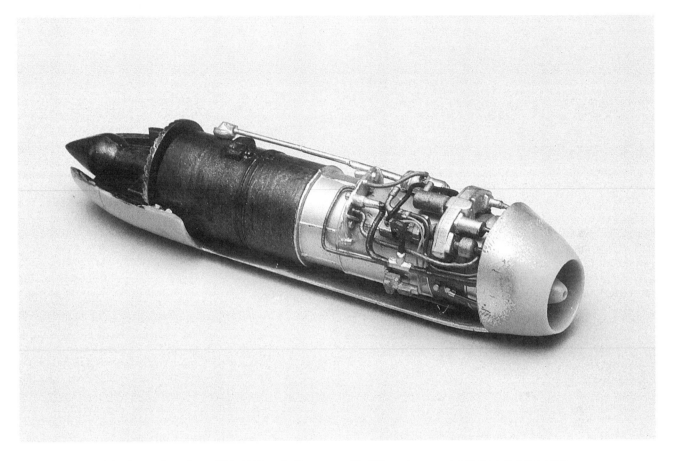

The forward section of this 1/48 scale Monogram Me 262 engine was detailed so that the open access panels would display a realistic-looking jet engine. (Model by Scott Weller.)

Detailing engines for propeller-driven aircraft includes adding wiring, piping, and cabling, as well as proper painting to highlight detail. You may also have to replace parts such as the valve push rods on radial engines because the kit-supplied parts don't match up with their locations on the cylinders; or you may have to add them if they weren't provided.

The amount of engine detailing you do depends on how you plan to build the model and display the engine, and whether it's a piston or jet engine. Jet engines don't offer as much detail opportunity, and most kit manufacturers don't include engines,

so all you are left with to work on are air intake and exhaust cone details. Unfortunately, these are sometimes lacking in the kit, but with the addition of small lengths of strip stock they can be greatly improved.

DETAILING ENGINES

Almost all radial engines have a ring-shaped wiring harness at the base of the crankcase. Spark plug wires emerge from this ring. Both ring and wires are protected by metal jackets. Most engines from the early '30s and later had two spark plug wires for each cylinder. They are located next to one another on the

ring with a wider space between sets of wires. One spark plug location was always centered on the front of the cylinder and the other either on the top or the back.

To add wiring you will need to mark the wiring harness ring for the correct number of cylinder sets and drill small holes in the ring with a pin vise and small drill bit for a positive seating. Use the circular template to match the ring to a circle size, draw it on paper, and mark the correct number of cylinders on the circle. This allows you to play with locations until you get them spaced evenly. Once you are satisfied with the spacing,

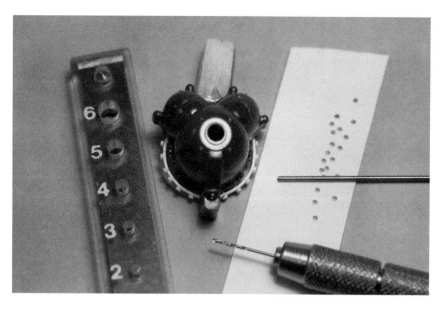

The wiring harness on Revell's 1/32 scale R-2800 engine was replaced and individual locations for the wiring were added using Waldron's punch tool.

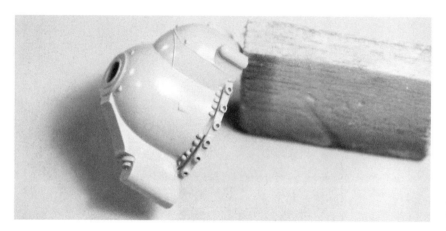

Drill out wiring locations so the strands of stretched plastic seat properly.

transfer the locations to the part using a small marker.

Now drill holes in the cylinders at the correct spark plug locations. Be sure the drill bit size matches the size of the wiring. Use strands of electronic wire for 1/48 and 1/72 scale engines, and stretched sprue for 1/32 and 1/24 scale kits. If you use electronic wire, strip the plastic covering off, separate the strands, and stretch them carefully to straighten them out.

After drilling the holes for the spark plug wires, prime the subassemblies and give them a coat of Testor's gloss gull gray. To accent cylinders and highlight cooling vanes, hand paint them with Testor's non-buffing gunmetal Metalizer. Testor's Metalizer paints are thinned for airbrushing, but the non-buffing types can be brushed onto small areas. Due to the thinned consistency of the paint and the fact that it doesn't adhere well to gloss enamels, the paint will flow into the areas between the cylinder's cooling vanes while only slightly staining the tops of the vanes. This gives a two-color appearance to the cylinders and highlights detail.

Be extra careful applying the Metalizer in the area where the cylinder meets the crankcase because thinned paint can easily flow onto the face of the crankcase. The tops of the cylinders are usually a darker color than the body, so paint them with Testor's non-buffing exhaust color Metalizer. To accent crankcase bolts use Testor's silver applied with a

Testor's Metalizer colors highlight the details of this engine. The base color was airbrushed and cylinder colors were applied with a brush.

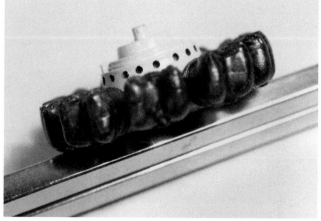

No push rods are supplied on Revell's 1/32 scale R-2800, but you can add them without much trouble. Drill the locations for the individual push rods using the cylinder locations as a guide.

sharpened round toothpick. As a final touch add a small square or rectangular black decal to the crankcase to represent the manufacturer's plate.

Push rods that are separate parts seldom match their locations on the cylinder heads. I recommend cutting them at their base and replacing them with Evergreen round plastic stock. Paint a length of round stock the correct color (black or natural metal), then cut approximate lengths for the number of push rods you need. Form-fit each push rod into place and attach with Elmer's white glue. Where the push rod meets the cylinder head the glue also acts as a filler that can be touched up with paint.

To weather the engine, dust it with a mixture of brown and black pastel applied with a soft brush and airbrush a coat of clear flat to seal. Drybrush some Polly-S "oil" color onto the engine cylinders and the area where the cylinders meet the crankcase. Apply a touch of Polly-S oil color to the crankcase sump, which is the long rectangular part protruding from the crankcase and pointing down. These oil stains must be subtle, so don't overdo it.

The last step is to add the wiring. Determine the color of the metal covering protecting the actual engine wiring: usually this was copper, black, or a bright metallic color. After you paint the wire strands or sprue, install them around the harness at the base of the crankcase using white glue. Form-fit them one cylinder location at a time. I usually do the front wires first, then locate the wires for the backs of the cylinders. If there is a second row of cylinders I work on the front row first.

In-line engines are set up much like straight block automobile engines—spark plug wires on both sides of the engine block in straight rows. Remove the molded wiring detail with a #11 X-Acto blade and sandpaper. Then mark the locations of the spark plug wires and drill holes. The spark plug wires are usually wrapped together and distributed along the block. Glue them one at a time and bundle them together as you

The wiring on this engine ended on the back side, where it would not be seen.

Airbrush the push rods with Testor's Metalizer and then cut and form-fit them into place. The engine part on the right is the stock kit part. What a difference a few lengths of plastic rod can make on an engine that lacks detail!

Hasegawa's 1/32 scale engine for its Peashooter kit is great, but the push rods don't line up with the cylinder heads. To correct these types of problems, simply remove the kit's rods and replace them with individual lengths.

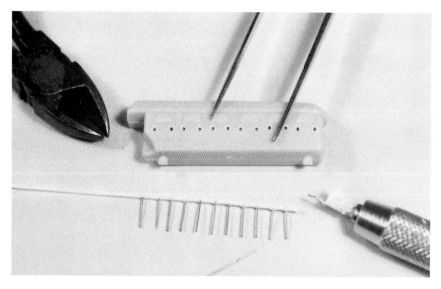

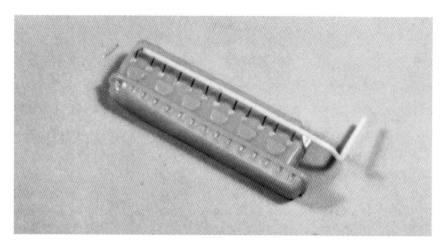

Even if the engine is molded into the fuselage, you can still add detail. To enhance the appearance of Monogram's 1/48 scale P-51 Mustang, wiring and drain tubes were added. (Model by Richard Boutin, Sr.)

(Left) Bundled stretched sprue or a combination of plastic rod and thin wire can represent wiring harnesses on in-line engines.

(Center) The wiring harness has been installed and will be painted after assembly of the rest of the engine. These details add a three dimensional effect to in-line engines.

move toward the rear of the engine. White glue works best because it dries clear.

Mixture, throttle, and sensor cables, as well as other types of wiring you may want to add to an engine, can be made by stretching various diameters and colors of sprue. Always start with a long length of sprue, glue one end in place, form-fit it into place, and then glue the other end.

To give the engine weight and to anchor the spark plug wires more securely, you may want to fill the block with resin. Be sure all seams are sealed, or the resin will seep out.

You can also highlight detail on these engines by painting them various shades and colors. The block is usually a different color than the top of the engine and rear components. Engine mounts are usually framing, which can be painted various shades of the same color.

The overall effect of adding wires, painting the engine and mounts different colors, and weathering is to turn even an average in-line engine into a masterpiece.

Jet engines are the most difficult to detail, and few models have them. The original piping and wiring are difficult to remove without marring the engine, so I recommend adding additional piping and wiring to provide a perception of depth. Evergreen rod is the best plastic for this because it is soft and flexible. Use various size rods, especially if you are running several lengths together, and always use Elmer's white glue to attach them to the engine. Thin electronics solder also works well because it conforms easily to the shape of the engine. Add junction boxes and other appendages using various sizes and shapes of small square stock. If you are going to connect piping and wiring to these junction boxes, drill small holes so the rods will fit into them.

Most engines, like the ones supplied with Hasegawa's 1/32 scale F-104 or Revell's 1/32 scale Me 262, have lots of molded-on detail which can be greatly enhanced by drybrushing. The molded boxes on these engines also make excellent connection points for additional piping and wiring.

You might also try sanding the backing of the intake part until only the vanes are left. Trace the part on sheet stock, cut it out, paint both parts, and position the circular disk about 1/16 inch (1.6 mm) behind the intake. This increase the perception of depth and makes the individual turbine blades stand out.

PROPELLERS, ENGINE INTAKES & EXHAUSTS

Proper painting of propellers should not be overlooked. After you remove the mold lines, give the propeller a coat of primer and mask the blades. Airbrush the tips gloss yellow with a few drops of gloss white added to make the color look faded. After it has dried (two to three days), mask these areas and paint the blades gloss black with a little gloss white added to make a slightly lighter shade. (If the hub area is a different color than the blades, mask it too.) Use gloss black because flat black does not accept a clear finish well. It will also ensure that small decals on the propeller blades will not silver.

Finally, mask the entire length of the blades before you spray the hubs. After you have finished painting,

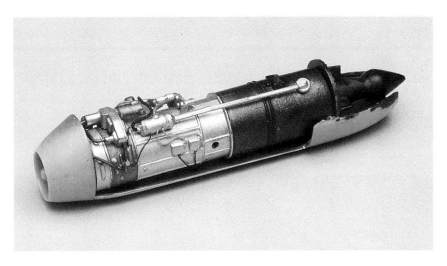

Adding tubing and wiring detail to jet engines takes time because you must conform the tubing to the shape of the engine. This 1/48 scale Me 262 engine by Monogram is a combination of kit parts, metal, and plastic tubing. (Model by Scott Weller.)

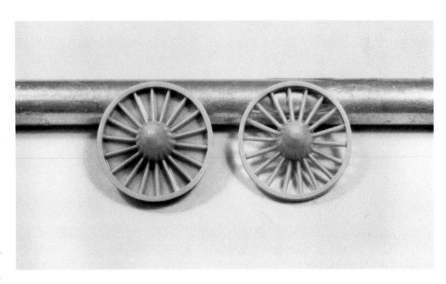

Improve the appearance of jet engine intakes by removing the plastic from around the turbine blades. This is done easily by running the part across a piece of sandpaper.

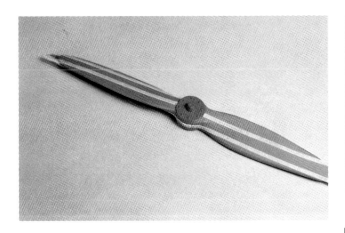

Masking propeller blades to represent laminated wood is easy with thin strips of masking tape.

Most metal propellers can be masked and painted quickly, but if you are using gloss paints, be sure they are dry before you mask them.

apply decals to the blades. When they have dried, run a soft lead pencil across the leading edges; then run your finger across the lead residue to work it into the paint and flatten it out. This will give the blades a subtly worn effect. Seal the residue by airbrushing the entire propeller with a clear flat finish.

Oil and grease leak out of the propeller hub where the pitch gears are located and smear onto the hub and down the blades. Although the oil is blown off during flight and splattered onto the engine and cowling, as the engine comes to a stop after landing the oil seeps onto the blades. It streaks across the front of the blades, but not all the way out to the tips. Generally the first quarter length has this residual oil, so use your Polly-S oil color sparingly in this area.

Frequently overlooked by modelers are engine exhaust ports, air intakes, cowling flaps, and other exterior engine vents. They are normally molded as solid pieces or have solid screen grating molded on. For a touch of realism, hollow them out.

Exhaust ports can be hollowed out in several ways, depending on the type of model and the locations of the ports. On a fighter plane they can be hollowed out with a Dremel drill press stand and a motor tool. Match the bit to the port diameters and drill out the plastic by pressing the part to the bit. The trick is to hold the part with both hands. Don't let the bit contact it for long or you may melt the plastic. Go slowly and drill small layers of plastic at a time. Remove the part frequently to check progress and blow away the plastic shavings.

For exhausts like those on bombers use combinations of drill bits and micro files to cut into the plastic and shape it. If the ports are oblong, use motor tool side cutters; when you get the pilot hole drilled, you can shape it easily with the side

Drilling out engine exhausts adds another level of realism to your model. The engine exhausts on Monogram's beautiful 1/48 scale B-25J were hollowed out using drill bits and micro files.

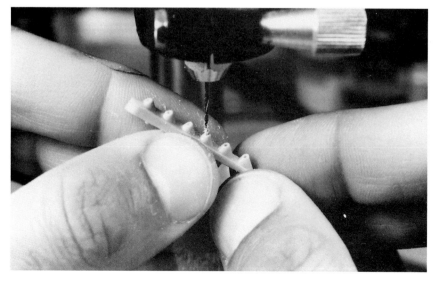

Open angled exhaust ports by holding them with both hands and carefully drilling out the individual ports.

(Right) Hollowing exhaust ports on kit-supplied parts makes a big improvement.

(Center) Sometimes cutters and drill bits are not enough to hollow out a part. In these stubborn cases use micro files to cut and shape.

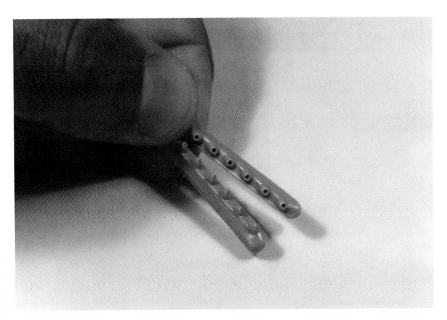

cutter. When hollowing out exhausts, go only deep enough so the port appears to be hollow—between $\frac{1}{16}$ and $\frac{1}{8}$ inch (1.6 mm and 3.2 mm).

Engine breather holes and intakes can be tricky, especially with multiple holes next to one another like those on a P-51 Mustang. For small holes use a pin vise with a drill bit to get the hole started to a good depth. Then if you decide to speed up the process with a motor tool the bit will have a good starter hole. Small bits tend to skip if the pilot hole is not deep enough. For square air intakes use micro files or a combination of files and bits to remove the plastic, shape the hole, and thin out the sides. Since you are working with thin plastic, be gentle and go slowly.

Cowling flaps, especially on a bomber, look more realistic if the plastic between them is removed. This can be done with a razor saw or a jeweler's saw, depending on the scale of the model. Generally, the smaller scales require a jeweler's saw.

Engine vents can also be drilled out several ways, depending on the situation. The most difficult are the small vents, especially on the upper wing surfaces of bombers. The best

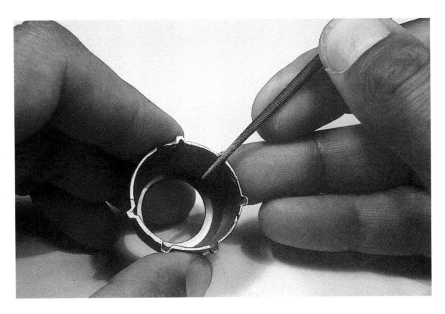

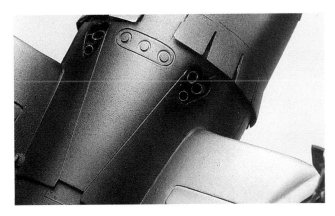

Sometimes you have to replace the exhausts with tubing. The molded in exhaust ports on Revell's 1/32 scale Corsair were cut out and replaced with plastic tubing. The edges were thinned with a #11 X-Acto blade.

Although photoetched parts are available for the breather holes on P-51 Mustangs, it's easier and cheaper to simply drill out the holes.

Another area that is sometimes overlooked by modelers is removing the plastic from between the cowling flaps. It can easily be done with a jeweler's saw.

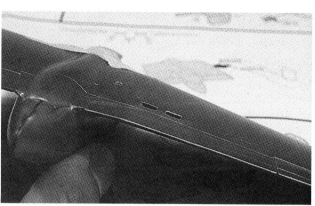

The wing vents on Monogram's 1/48 scale B-25J were drilled out and cleaned and shaped with a #11 X-Acto blade. Protect surrounding plastic with masking tape first.

way to hollow them out is to drill a series of small holes, use a #11 X-Acto blade to remove the plastic between them, and smooth the sides with micro files. There is little room for error, and repairing gouges can be difficult in some locations. Mask the surrounding plastic so it will not be damaged if you slip.

To remove large amounts of plastic, start small and progressively enlarge the diameter and depth of the hole. This is slow going, but you can achieve thin plastic walls without melting them if you work up to the size you want. To secure a part in a vise, sandwich it between two pieces of balsa wood for protection. The balsa will also help hold it in place.

Air intakes can be open or have screening covers, so check your documentation. Fighters usually have big air intakes on the front of the cowling or around the front of the fuselage, while two- and four-engine bombers can have intakes on the leading edges of the wings as well. If the area is covered with screening, cut out the molded screening and add photo-etched screening. Not all air intakes on an aircraft have screen covers; a good example is the B-17. The intakes between the engines have screening, while those between the fuselage and inboard engines don't.

Model Technologies and other photoetching companies market excellent grades of wire mesh screen-

ing. It can be hard to cut to an exact shape, so plan placement carefully and use an oversized section. Cut it to the approximate shape and install it on the inside of either the fuselage or the wing. This requires some patience because you need to form-fit by trial and error, but it sure beats trying to cut it to the exact size and installing it from the outside.

Exhaust ports generally take on a rust or mud color due to temperature and exposure to the elements. Paint exhausts with Testor's burnt metal buffing Metalizer, polish with a Q-Tip, and seal with Testor's Metalizer sealer so the color is dulled. I have seen real B-17s with exhausts that appear to be almost a mud color.

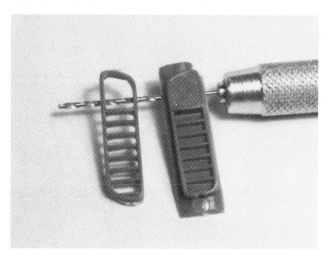

One of the toughest engine intake parts to scratchbuild is a Corsair intake, but there is an easier way. Run the part across a dowel wrapped with sandpaper until the backing is very thin, and remove the remaining plastic with a knife.

Once the part is cleaned up add photoetched screening and glue it in place. Super glue works best as a filler, especially to shape parts around small areas.

THE FLIGHT LINE

A6M5 Zero manufactured by Hasegawa, Inc. (1/48 scale kit built by Major Billy Crisler, USAF.)

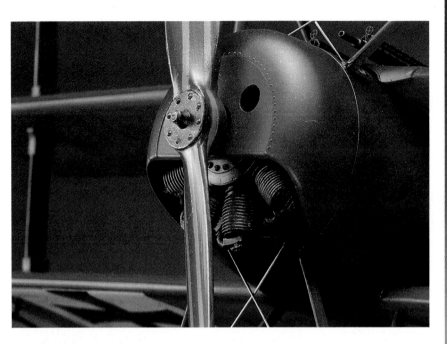

Fokker Triplane manufactured by Revell, Inc. (1/28 scale kit built by Mike Ashey.)

A-7E Corsair II manufactured by Hasegawa, Inc. (1/48 scale kit built by Major Billy Crisler, USAF.)

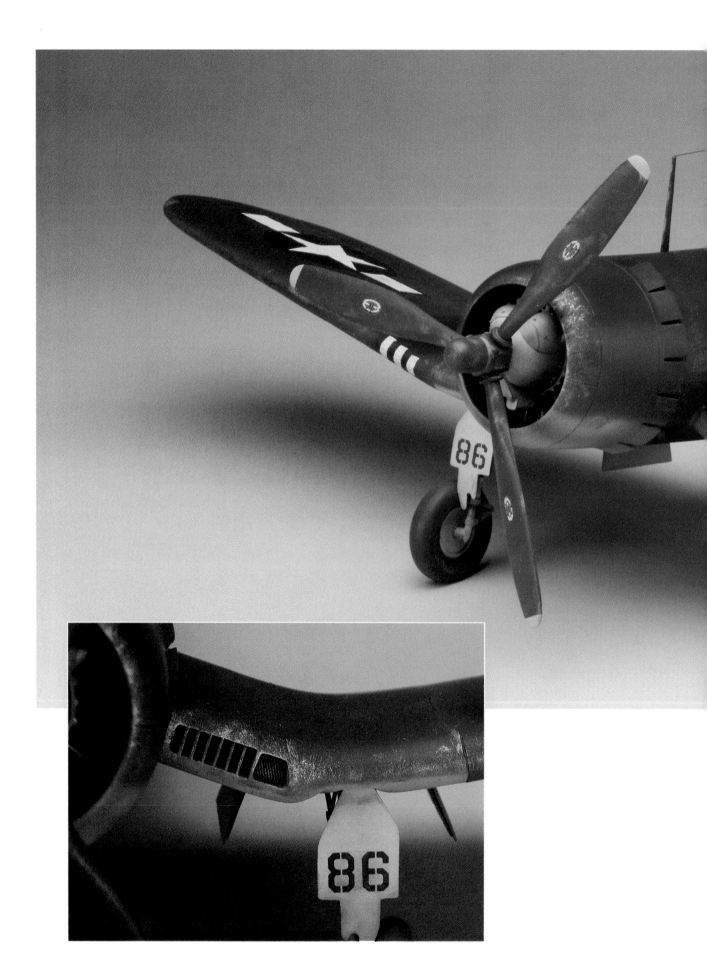

F4U-1 Corsair
manufactured by Revell, Inc.
(1/32 scale kit built by Mike Ashey.)

Boeing P-12E manufactured by Hasegawa, Inc. (1/32 scale kit built by Mike Ashey.)

P-51 Mustang manufactured by Hasegawa, Inc. (1/32 scale kit built by Mike Ashey.)

B-25J Mitchell manufactured by Monogram, Inc. (1/48 scale kit built by Mike Ashey.)

Actuator rod, hydraulic lines, and wiring were added to the back side of the forward and rear walls of Monogram's 1/48 scale Prowler. Adding parts like this is easy. All you need is a picture of the actual interior and five cents worth of plastic rod and electronics wire. (Model by Scott Weller.)

(Left, above) No instrument decals were used in Monogram's 1/48 scale Prowler. The overall effect of good painting technique and the use of different shades and colors differentiated the individual instrument boxes, switches, and dials. (Model by Scott Weller.)

(Left) Although Monogram's 1/48 scale Prowler already has a great interior, the throttle quadrant was enhanced with the addition of larger levers. (Model by Scott Weller.)

F-100 Super Sabre manufactured by Monogram, Inc. (1/48 scale kit built by Scott Weller.)

A-10 Thunderbolt manufactured by Monogram, Inc. (1/48 scale kit built by Scott Weller.)

Grumman F3F manufactured by Monogram, Inc. (1/32 scale kit built by Mike Ashey.)

P-51 Mustang manufactured by Monogram, Inc. (1/48 scale kit built by Richard Boutin, Jr.)

Grumman J2F-2 Duck manufactured by Glenco, Inc. (1/48 scale kit built by Mike Ashey.)

P-40 Warhawk manufactured by Revell, Inc. (1/32 scale kit built by Mike Ashey.)

P-26 Peashooter manufactured by Hasegawa, Inc. (1/32 scale kit built by Mike Ashey.)

(Right) There is no substitute for the air intakes on this Corsair. All it took to achieve this level of realism is a little elbow grease and about ten cents worth of photoetched screening.

(Center) The exhaust stains stand out against the faded appearance of the olive drab paint. Note the subtle exhaust stains on the upper surfaces of the elevators, caused by the two inboard engines. (Model by Richard Boutin, Sr.)

Although this might be the actual color, on small scale models it just doesn't look right.

Jet exhaust nozzles are complex pieces of equipment that can expand and contract depending on speed and acceleration. The nozzles are designed along the same principles as a camera's diaphragm. The diaphragm is a series of metal plates that slide past one another to form an opening of a specific size. On jet nozzles this can be represented by gluing small strips of plastic stock along the nozzle's interior and exterior. When adding stock, do a test run and glue the strips with small amounts of Elmer's white glue. The trial run will tell you a lot about the spacing you need between strips. Once you get the spacing set, you can make a spacer out of a piece of strip or sheet stock. It will ensure evenly spaced strips around the nozzle. If you have an odd spacing, position that area toward the bottom. To remove strips, soak the part in water.

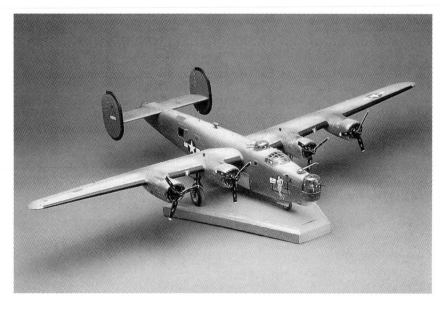

You can also add the actuator rods that move the plates, but I recommend this only on 1/32 scale aircraft. On 1/48 and 1/72 scale kits just adding the strips to both sides of the nozzle will give the parts the appearance of depth. Paint the nozzle with Testor's buffing Metalizer and use a Q-Tip to polish it. The Q-Tip will only touch the top areas of the strip, resulting in a two-tone effect.

Don't forget to paint the insides of the cowling, the engine compartment, and any air intakes and

Adding small plastic strips on both the outside and inside of a jet exhaust can greatly improve its appearance. (Model by Major Billy Crisler, USAF.)

exhausts the correct colors. Engine compartments are usually covered in exhaust stains, grease, and oil stains, and the engine mounting framing is usually discolored by heat, so be sure to paint these details. The outer areas of engine brackets usually acquire a slightly burnt metal appearance, so add some Testor's burnt metal Metalizer to these areas. Dust the engine compartment with a dark pastel and seal it with Polly-S clear flat before you add any oil or grease stains. Wash the interior corners and folds with Polly-S oil color and dry-brush the interior surface with a combination of Polly-S oil and flat black. Jet exhausts are usually a mixture of burnt metal shades, which can be achieved using Testor's buffing and non-buffing Metalizers.

The tail areas of jets usually have several shades of burnt metal due to the intense heat created by the engine. Different mixtures of Testor's Metalizer were used to achieve the various shades on the tail area of this model. The various shades were blended in with a Q-Tip. (Model by Scott Weller.)

CHAPTER FOUR

LANDING GEAR, BAYS & DOORS

The landing gear bays on Revell's 1/32 scale Corsair are pretty much void of detail, but the addition of plastic sheeting and strip stock turned them into highly detailed replicas.

Detailing landing gear is not as time-consuming as working on cockpits and engines, but many modelers overlook these areas because they spend so much time on the big stuff. Landing gear bays and doors, for instance, are sometimes overlooked. In the smaller scales you can get away with painting detail on the insides of the doors, but 1/48 and 1/32 scale aircraft call for extra work.

Detail provided by manufacturers for landing gear bays varies widely. If the model has no landing gear bay, you can build one and add as much detail as you want. To con-struct the box accurately you will have to draw the area to be boxed in on the inside of the upper wing. I recommend attaching the sides of the new landing gear bay to the upper wing, because it is easier to add detail to the boxed-in area if it is attached to the upper rather than the lower wing. To accurately draw the outline of the lower wing's opening onto the upper wing, tape them together and draw the outline, using a lead pencil with its lead long enough to allow you to follow the edge of the opening accurately. Since most landing gear bays are larger than the opening on the lower wing, enlarge the drawing on the upper wing slightly.

Now determine the interior contours of the sides of the landing gear bay that run from the leading edge to the trailing edge of the wing. Since wings are tapered, the sides are different shapes, so you will have to measure and cut two separate sections. The most accurate method for determining interior wing contours is to cut up a second model and use it as a form guide for the interior areas.

Draw the locations of the sides of the landing gear bay onto the outer surfaces of the second model's wing,

(Left) Even if you only add some sheet stock to form an interior landing gear bay, you will improve your model's appearance. It certainly looks better than just having a hole on the underside of the wing.

(Center) Using a second kit to get the exact interior wing contours for the areas around the landing gear bay is easier than trying to form-fit these types of scratchbuilt parts. The wing on this kit has been cut up, so interior contours along cut lines can be transferred to sheet stock.

glue the wings together, and cut it into sections along the lines with a razor saw. Run a grease pencil along the edge of the cut line, impress it onto sheet stock, and cut out the part.

To check the fit of the interior section use small pieces of tape to hold the part in place and tape the leading or trailing edge of the wing so you can open and close it like a hinged box. This will allow you to check the fit and make any adjustments. The interior part should fit almost perfectly. Once you have both sides of the new landing gear bay installed you can easily do the front and back areas, because their exact heights will be defined for you. All you have to do is transfer the measurements with a pair of dividers to some sheet stock, cut out the required shape, and install it.

Since cutting the wing area of the second model puts a lot of stress on the glue joints, you may want to install some interior bracing so it won't flex once you cut it. When installing braces, be careful not to change the shape of the wing by installing one that is too big, and be sure to use super glue. Also, cut the area closest to the fuselage first, transfer the shape, cut it out, test-fit it, and then cut the wing along the outer location. Since the thickness of the plastic may vary between wings, and since one wing may have an interior contour slightly different than the

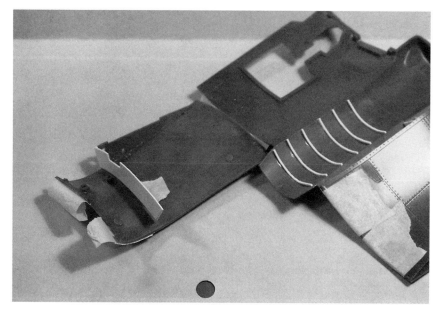

Before you start adding interior parts, draw their locations on the inside of the wing area. Add one part at a time and check the fit of each part.

The landing gear bays on this Corsair have been completed. Adding one part at a time and duplicating your work on both wing areas as you go will help ensure that both areas look the same.

As you build up the landing gear bay, you can start adding other interior parts such as framing.

other, cut up both wings and fit each one individually.

If your model has its landing gear bay within the fuselage, follow the same procedure, except you would be cutting the second model's fuselage instead of the wings. Some older jet kits have no landing gear bays, but they can be easily added using this technique.

Once the boxed-in area is complete you can add interior framing along the sides, front, and bottom. Use a small section of sheet stock with one straight edge to draw lines wherever you want to install framing. Doing so will ensure that the strip stock is evenly spaced and straight. There is no set size for each scale, but I recommend installing plastic strips that look accurate. Cut long lengths so you can position them correctly, and use a thin wire applicator to apply glue.

Once you have the sides installed you can form-fit the strips along the bottom. Form-fit them tightly one at a time and glue where the bottom framing meets the side framing. The super glue will seep

Sometimes all you have to do to improve the appearance of a landing gear bay is add some extra plastic to the kit-supplied-detail. The framing was form-fitted into place and the holes were punched using Waldron's punch tool. (Model by Richard Boutin, Sr.)

along the underside of the bottom strip, securing it. When the framing is complete, paint the area and add weathering. Give landing gear bays a dusting of various colors of pastels, then seal with a clear flat finish.

The last step is to add interior piping. You can use Evergreen rod, stiff wire, or thin solder. If you run several lengths close together, make them different sizes for the added effect of depth. Whether you are running piping from front to back or left to right, drill holes through the sides of the landing gear bay and slide the tubing into place through the holes.

This looks realistic and you don't have to be accurate when you cut the rod lengths. Paint the lengths before you install them. If they are all the same color, use different shades. For small paint jobs like tubing, use water-base paints because they dry quickly. You can mix the various shades of paint in a bottle cap, clean it out, and mix another shade. Finally, apply a dusting of pastel on the piping.

If the manufacturer has supplied a landing gear bay but it cries out for additional detail, you can add it the same way you added piping detail to a scratch-built box. If you need to add

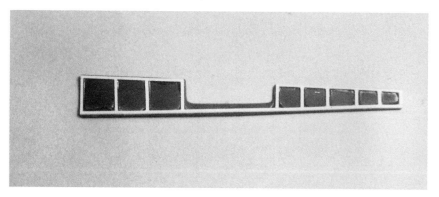

The addition of some strip stock can greatly enhance the appearance of a wheel well door that has no detail.

The new interior sheeting for the landing gear doors is attached by running a bead of super glue around its perimeter with a thin wire applicator. The hinges were made with Waldron's punch set.

framing, be consistent with the locations of the strips. Sometimes manufacturers supply molded framing that is not high enough or is not accurate. You can add additional framing by form-fitting individual pieces, but again, be consistent. The best way to glue these pieces is to set them in place and put a small drop of super glue at each corner. Once the glue is dry, run a bead along the contact area to blend the two together.

Wiring and piping detail that has been molded into the landing gear bay can be difficult to paint. Even if you do a superb job, it may not look quite right. In these instances I paint the entire area one color and apply a lighter wash of the same color to highlight the molded detail. Additionally, I select a different color pastel to further highlight these details. To create a good perception of depth and help offset the appearance that the cabling and tubing are molded into the plastic, add some additional piping and cabling painted a different color or a much lighter shade of the color of the interior area of the bay. You are trying for a three-dimensional effect, and additional detail will go a long way toward this.

If the landing gear doors have no detail, you can add some sheet stock or strips. The doors of actual aircraft landing gear have either a framing covered with thin metal sheeting or a sandwiched sheet with an outer skin and an inner skin that has been drop-formed by a heavy press. Whether the aircraft doors have framing or inner sheeting, thin the doors for realism. If they have flat surfaces, run them across a stationary piece of sandpaper. If they are curved, use a wooden dowel of the appropriate diameter with sandpaper wrapped around it.

To add framing, draw the locations of the strips onto the door. Be sure the outer framing that follows the perimeter of the door is slightly offset from the door's lip. Check your documentation for the approximate design and duplicate it. It does not have to be exact—you just need to approximate the appearance.

Run a bead of super glue along the contact surface of the strip, and set it along one of the lines you've drawn. Plan your gluing so you can use extra-long strips as much as possible, since they can be cut to size once the glue has set. After you have placed all the strips, paint the inner doors the correct color and lightly weather them using pencil pastels and a flat brush.

If the doors have an inner sheeting, chances are there are circular or elongated perforations in it. On actual aircraft these holes add strength and reduce weight. Place the door onto the sheeting you want to use and trace the outline. If the doors are curved, tape a piece of sheeting around the same wood dowel you used to thin the part and trace. This will give you the exact size. Next, draw the locations of any holes onto the area you traced, using templates and triangles. For any half-circles or circles, select a template size that is the same as a Waldron punch. Waldron's punch set can be used on 1/24 to 1/72 scale doors. Although using it might not give you the exact size, no one will notice and it sure makes cutting easier.

Once you have the drawing set up on the outline, cut it out and punch or cut out the holes. Run the new part across some fine sandpaper to eliminate burrs and remove sanding fuzz from the holes. Place it on the inner surface of the landing door and run a bead of super glue along the perimeter of the combined parts. Be sure the contact surfaces are clean.

After the glue has dried, sand the sides smooth. The glue should have seeped far enough along the contact surface area between the parts to hold them tightly together. If a section bulges out, drill a small hole through the surface of the inner sheeting and place a drop of glue on the hole. Once the glue is dry, run the surface across sandpaper to smooth it. Paint the inside and then weather as necessary.

The inside of landing gear doors never gets direct sunlight so paint does not fade, but these surfaces usually have lubricants, fluids, and dirt on them from the landing gear, so add this type of weathering. Even modern jets suffer from dirty interiors.

A final note: Whether you are drawing framing or location holes, set up the actual door on the sheet stock outline to locate framing or holes accurately. To do this, set your triangles as you did for making consoles.

The last details to add to landing gear doors are the door actuators. They can either be mechanical arm devices that act like hinges, or hydraulic actuators with extending arms. For hinge-type actuators use strip stock of various sizes to build up the arms. Each door normally would have at least one hinge-type actuator. If the actuators are hydraulic, they are easy to make out of various size plastic tubing, plastic stock, or wire, depending on the scale.

For 1/24 and 1/32 scale kits you can use hollow tubing and solid rod, while 1/48 and 1/72 scales require

Monogram packed a lot of detail into their 1/48 scale F9F Panther. Although extra detailing is not really needed, a careful paint job can highlight all the details, such as the actuator arms. (Model by Major Billy Crisler, USAF.)

small diameter plastic rod and wire. For large scale kits use hollow tubing for the outer section and insert solid rod into the hollow tubing. If you have to use solid rod and wire, drill a pilot hole into the rod to give the wire a positive seating. You are trying to achieve an effect, and you may have to sacrifice some realism and accuracy when installing these parts.

LANDING GEAR STRUTS & WHEELS

The first step in detailing landing gear struts is to remove seam lines

and fill in ejection marks and dimples. If the strut has scissor-type framing that extends outward around the oleo (shock absorber) and connects the upper and lower strut, check your documentation to see if it is made of solid pieces of metal. Chances are this scissor-type device, which is designed to add strength to the landing gear strut, is made of metal framing. Draw the framing onto the solid sections and cut out the excess plastic. Start with a pilot hole, enlarge it with a #11 X-Acto blade and shape it with micro files.

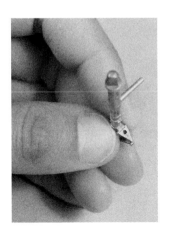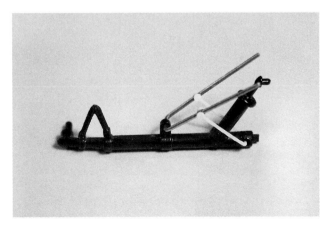

The first step in removing small amounts of plastic is to drill a pilot hole. The interior plastic will be removed so that a frame is formed.

Sometimes you just can't salvage landing gear parts and you have to scratchbuild them. A combination of wire and plastic rod has been added to this landing gear.

Prepare the strut and any other parts for painting, and mask the oleo portion of the strut. The oleo is the airplane's shock absorber. It pushes up into the strut and is usually a shiny metal, which can be represented with Testor's Metalizer paints. I usually use three shades of the same color paint for struts. Although this requires a lot of masking, the results are worth it. The area above the oleo gets one shade, the area below the oleo gets the second, and any remaining parts, such as landing gear strut supports, get the third. The tones should be subtle, but viewers should be able to pick up detail on the landing gear through color differentiation. Mask the lower area when you paint the upper strut area. Then let the paint dry and reverse the process.

Additional landing gear strut pieces can be painted separately.

Once the struts and accessories are painted, remove the tape from the oleo area and mask the entire strut. Airbrush the oleo with Testor's aluminum buffing Metalizer. After the paint is dry, use a Q-Tip to polish the Metalizer, then carefully remove the tape. Next, attach any additional parts to the struts. To position the parts correctly, you may have to fit the strut into its wing location and then attach the parts to the strut.

Next, identify how hydraulic brake lines are attached to the landing gear strut. To make brake lines I use black plastic sprue stretched over a candle for flexible lines, and piano wire for stiff metal hydraulic lines, such as the ones on a B-25. The brake lines usually terminate near the axle or somewhere on the backside of the wheel hub. I locate the termination point, drill a small hole, place a small drop of Kristal Kleer or Elmer's white glue in the hole and insert the brake line. If the brake line is flexible, bend the end toward the strut after the glue has dried so it follows the length of the strut. The majority of brake lines are attached to the landing gear struts with thin flexible clamps like those on the cooling hoses for your car's radiator. You can simulate them by using a thin strip of masking tape laid over itself one time. There are usually two or three of these clamps on each strut. I always work from the brake line termination point up towards the top of the strut so I can work out any excessive slack in the line. Apply a small drop of super glue at the point where the tape ends. Paint the tape with Polly-S aluminum colored paint.

The last step is to add weathering and oil leaks. Dust the entire landing gear with a dark pastel color, and airbrush a coat of Polly-S clear flat to seal the pastel dust. Be careful not to get the clear flat finish onto the oleo because it will dull the shiny appearance of the paint. Oleos usually have hydraulic fluid stains that start at the top and streak downward. Simulate this effect with Polly-S oil-colored

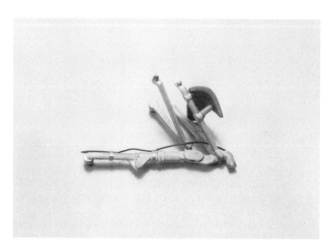

Hydraulic brake lines were added to Monogram's 1/32 scale F3F.

(Right) Oleos leak hydraulic fluid, so don't forget this subtle detail. Thinned water-base paints work best for this.

(Center) For spokes that are clean and uniform, clean the excess plastic from the inside of the wheel.

paint applied with a small brush. Finally, position and glue the landing gear struts into place without the wheels.

Most main landing gear wheels don't have solid wheel hubs, but kit manufacturers are forever molding solid wheel hubs with indented spoke detail or molding round or oblong indentations. You'll need to remove the plastic between the spokes.

Begin by drilling a starter hole in the area to be removed and enlarge it with a #11 X-Acto blade. The raised plastic that represents the spokes will guide your blade, but be careful not to gouge these areas. Use micro files to shape the outline of the hollow area and smooth out the sides. These files are especially helpful for the curved portions of the hollow area. After you have finished removing the plastic, clean off the excess on the inside of the wheel.

For hubs with round indentations use a drill bit of the same diameter as the indentation. Since the plastic is usually thick, deepen the indentations with a drill bit and pin vise and finish drilling with a motor tool. Oblong holes are a little harder, and if you're working in 1/48 or smaller, just drill them out with a bit that will cover the oblong shape.

For 1/32 scale kits you can get the oblong shape using a combination of drill bits, cutters, and micro files. First, punch an indentation in the center for positive seating and drill out as much of the plastic as possible with a bit that will touch the narrow distance of the oblong shape. This will leave small portions of plastic on both sides which can be removed with a micro file. Install the motor tool in a drill press; then you can control the cutting action by moving the wheel along the base of the drill press.

You can deal with odd-shaped areas by starting a pilot hole and then enlarging it.

(Left) The completed wheel, primed and ready to paint, is a far cry from the stock part supplied by the manufacturer.

(Center) The spoked wheels on this 1/32 scale Corsair add another element of realism to the overall effect of the model, thanks to a small investment in drill bits and micro files.

Once you have completed both sides of a wheel, sand the gluing surfaces smooth by sliding the part along sandpaper; then glue them together. When you glue, be sure the spokes or holes on both wheel halves match so you can see through the hub.

After the glue has dried, scrape the seam with a #11 X-Acto blade and sand smooth. Check your work by painting the area with silver paint. If you find any cracks, apply super glue and sand smooth. Unfortunately, doing this also removes any tread detail the manufacturer may have provided along the seam line, but it can be replaced. Place the wheel in a vise between two pieces of balsa wood to protect the plastic and take a thin razor saw or jeweler's saw and cut the tread detail back into the wheel.

For 1/32 scale and larger kits, use either the razor saw or the jeweler's saw, but for 1/48 scale and smaller use the jeweler's saw. Replacing or cutting new tread is slow work, and you must rotate the wheel continually in the vise.

Be careful to match the tread patterns. Because the new tread will be deeper, use the existing tread as a guide. Cut these areas deeper to match. When you are done, remove the wheel and sand with 600 grit sandpaper to remove plastic burrs.

Apply a coat of primer to the entire wheel. After it dries, mask the rim. Don't paint the rim black because you will have a hard time covering it, especially with a light color. Next, take a round toothpick or a .5mm lead pencil and run the tip around the edge of the rim where it meets the tire. The tape will stick to

This tire would look pretty strange with the center section of tread missing. Jeweler's saws are excellent tools for replacing tread detail.

the rim and define where tire meets rim. Carefully run a #11 X-Acto blade along the base of the rim using the rim as a guide. It is important that the blade runs along the base of the rim where it meets the tire. Remove excess tape and run the toothpick around the rim again to ensure that the tape is sticking. Repeat the procedure for the other side and airbrush the tire with flat black with some white mixed in for a dark gray.

After the paint has dried, remove the tape and mask the side of the wheel, but be sure it overlaps the tire. Again, trace the rim with a round toothpick or .5mm lead pencil, and cut it around the base of the rim. This time remove the tape that covers the rim and run the toothpick around the remaining tape one more time to ensure that it is sticking. Repeat the procedure for the other side. Cover any areas of the tire that aren't masked. Paint the hub the required color, let dry, and carefully remove the tape. Look for a fine demarcation line between tire and rim. Since you painted the lighter color last, if any paint bled over it will be the lighter onto the darker, which can be fixed easily with a detail brush. To add a touch of dirt to the hubs, apply a dusting of black pastel with a soft brush, then airbrush a coat of clear flat to seal.

After you have finished the tires, scrape the paint off the strut axles and position the tires on the axles. Once you have a proper alignment, carefully turn the model over and place a drop of super glue on the contact surface between the strut axle and the wheel rim.

The last step is to flatten each tire slightly so it appears to be supporting weight. I use an iron for this.

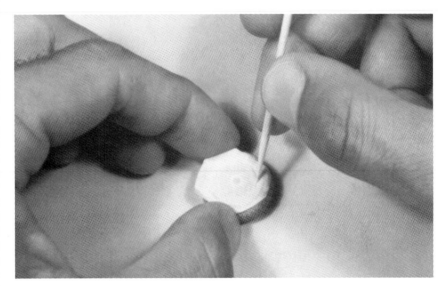

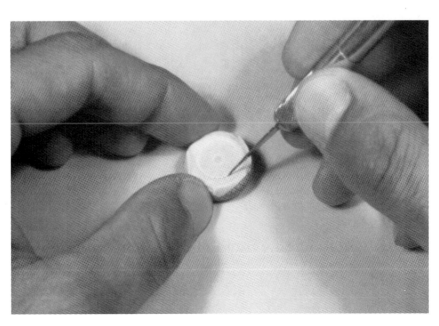

Tires can be given a bulged or flattened appearance by placing them onto a hot iron, but this effect needs to be very subtle. Don't leave the plastic on the iron too long, or you will end up with a flat tire instead of one that appears to be supporting the weight of the aircraft.

To prevent the plastic from sticking to the iron put a small piece of butcher's waxed paper between the tire and the iron. The waxed side of the paper should be touching the plastic. Lay the iron next to the side of your workbench so the side is flush with the bench. Position the model, one wheel at a time, onto the iron and watch the wheel as it begins to soften and lose its round shape. Putting some pressure on the wing area directly above the landing gear helps the wheel bulge out, but be very careful not to let it flatten too far or it will look like a blown-out tire. Don't forget to flatten the tail wheel.

If you don't have sharp lines between the rim and the tire you will ruin the realism, so be careful when painting. The landing gear on this 1/32 scale P-51 also has weathering, which can sometimes hide minor flaws.

CHAPTER FIVE

GUNS, FLYING WIRES, CONTROL CABLES & ANTENNA WIRES

Hollowing out the kit-supplied guns on Hasegawa's 1/32 scale P-51 adds another level of realistic detail.

Gunsight rings, front sight posts, ammo belts, and hollowed out guns add considerable realism to your models. Even if you do nothing but hollow out the gun, you will achieve an appreciable level of detail. Biplanes are one of my favorite modeling subjects; the flying wires and exterior control cables add an extra dimension and challenge. In addition, the biplanes of the golden age of aviation—the mid '20s to late '30s—had beautiful color schemes. Modeling these aircraft requires some specific construction techniques, especially when adding flying wires and control cables.

GUNS

The single most important detail you can add to guns is to hollow them out. Since these parts can become fragile after drilling, especially in the smaller scales, do all cleaning, scraping, and sanding before drilling. Don't paint the parts, though, until you have finished drilling, to avoid marring the paint finish. When you drill, be sure the surface in contact with the drill bit—in this case, the tip of the gun—is smooth and flat, so the bit will not skew off to one side.

Match the drill bit with the diameter of the part. Start with a small bit

and work up to the diameter you want. Progressively increase the bit size until you have the desired opening and depth. If you use too large a bit, the plastic wall that is formed as you drill may become too thin and collapse or fracture.

Place the part between two strips of balsa wood with about ½ inch (12.7 mm) of the gun barrel protruding from the wood. Press the strips together, place in the vise, and tighten just enough to prevent slippage. By pressing the balsa strips together you will push the ridges of the gun into the balsa, which will prevent it from moving.

(Left) On small scale models the contact surface for the drill bit is small, so use your drill press and vise to steady your drilling.

(Center) For large scale kits you can discard the vise and hollow out the part by punching it up to the drill bit.

Place the vise onto the drill press base and raise it to the motor tool until the bit and plastic are next to one another. This will allow you to adjust the part so it is straight and parallel with the drill bit.

Adjust the height of the motor tool above the vise. Ideally it should be adjusted so the bit will drill 1/16 to 1/8 inch (1.6 to 3.2 mm) into the plastic. Center the bit onto the plastic part. To ensure that the bit and part are centered, turn on the motor tool at its lowest speed and carefully drill a slight indentation into the part just deep enough to see. If it appears to be off-center, adjust the position of the vise and repeat.

Once the bit is centered, set the motor tool at its lowest speed. Don't let the bit come in contact with the plastic for more than a few seconds at a time. Apply slight, steady pressure. If you push too hard and try to finish the job all at once you will melt the plastic and ruin the part. You may find that during drilling a thin layer of melted plastic has covered the tip of the drill bit. It can be easily removed with a knife, but it is an indication that you are drilling too fast.

Another technique is to set up the motor tool in the drill press and hollow out the part by holding it with both hands and feeding the part up to the drill bit. This works well on 1/32 scale gun barrels. If you drill off to one side, you can correct the problem by installing a drill bit in a pin vise and drilling at an angle. The shaft of the bit must touch the thicker side; as you turn the bit the plastic will be shaved off. You can also use the tip of a #11 X-Acto blade to remove excess plastic, and use a bit in a pin vise to clean up the hollow area.

You can also hollow out the shell ejection ports on fighter planes. Most fighter plane kits have pronounced indentations in the lower wings for these ports, but they are not hollow.

If you can't use the kit-supplied guns, replace them with hollow plastic or metal rod. These guns on Monogram's 1/48 scale Panther are made of brass tubing painted with Testor's Metalizer. (Model by Major Billy Crisler, USAF.)

(Right) To hollow out shell ejection ports, drill starter holes into the plastic. Be sure to protect the surrounding wing area with masking tape in case you slip.

(Center) Once you enlarge the holes, use micro files to remove the remaining plastic and shape the openings.

Drill a starter hole and enlarge it with a #11 X-Acto blade. The molded plastic sides of the ports will provide a guide for the knife blade, but be careful not to damage these areas. Once the holes are enlarged, you can use your micro files to remove the remaining plastic.

For guns on bombers, I recommend adding gunsight rings and front sight aiming posts to the guns. Model Technologies makes excellent gunsight rings which are easy to install with a small drop of super glue. Front sight aiming posts can be made from stretched sprue. Ammo belts for the single guns in the nose or along the fuselage of a bomber can be added by using the 1/48 scale gun belts from Monogram's Huey Hog kit. Because they are in a double row, the kit's ammo belts must be split in half. Given some additional scraping, shaping, and painting, they make a fine addition.

Another detail is to attach the middle of some thin clear stretched sprue to the back of each gun and attach both ends to the interior wall of the bomber. This represents the bungee cord that held the guns stationary and helped support some of the weight. If you are planning to expose the gun bay areas of fighter planes with guns in their wings, add gun trigger cables to each, as well as cable sensors for counting the number of rounds remaining. The gun locations on aircraft kits such as Hasegawa's 1/32 scale F6F Hellcat or P51 also beg for added detail such as wiring and gun trigger cables.

When you are ready to paint, use Testor's buffing Metalizer gun metal. Spray on two coats and polish with a Q-Tip. The cotton tip will polish only

On this 1/48 scale B-24 machine gun the front sight post is made from stretched sprue. (Model by Richard Boutin, Sr.)

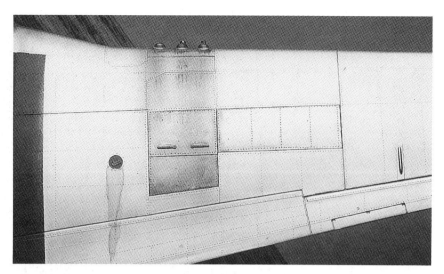

Gunpowder marks streak the wings of fighter planes and can range from subtle discolorations to heavy stains. The best way to replicate these is with diluted water-based paints applied with an airbrush.

Fighter aircraft that operated from dirt fields usually had covers over their gun ports to protect them from dust and dirt which could jam the guns. Small cuts of masking tape make excellent covers.

the larger raised surface areas, resulting in a two-tone appearance. This will also highlight the cooling hole detail along the gun barrel. Ammo belts need two separate colors—the shells were brass and the bullets were a dull bronze. Metal ammo drums were usually flat black, gray, or interior green, while those found on B-17s were wood. Be sure to add weathering to the interior areas where guns are located. These areas had stains from gun lubricant and cleaning solvent, as well as gunpowder.

BIPLANE FLYING WIRES & CONTROL CABLES

Biplanes require special construction techniques because you are dealing with multiple wing levels and wing struts that must be properly positioned. Many biplane kits have fit problems with the struts and the upper wing; the best way to detect this is to assemble the wings and struts with masking tape to see how they fit and how they are positioned. I usually build the fuselage and attach the lower wings first. Next I build the upper wing, and finally set the struts and upper wing with masking tape. In most instances you can solve a positioning problem by moving the upper wing, but doing so may also affect the struts. Both wings must be positioned correctly with respect to the fuselage. For this reason I recommend that you use masking tape to get set up correctly before you glue the struts and the upper wing.

Photoetched parts for World War I guns, available from IPMS, are worth the investment. The back half of this 1/28 scale gun was used instead of scratchbuilding the entire rear assembly.

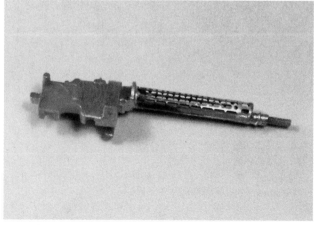

The fully assembled machine gun, complete with its barrel and sights, is now ready for a good coat of Testor's Metalizer paint.

Biplanes need special attention, especially when you are checking the fit of the wings and struts. This biplane is getting an initial fit check to ensure that the wings will sit correctly.

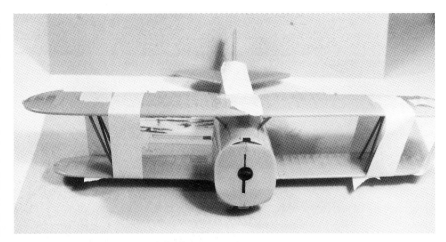

Another good reason to attach the struts and upper wing with masking tape is to examine how to install the flying wires. Once the wings and struts are glued, especially on 1/48 and 1/72 scale kits, there is not a lot of room to work between them; it's a good idea to see how tough it's going to be to get flying wires installed in areas such as between the fuselage and upper wing. In addition, if the manufacturer did not mark locations where flying wires need to be, you will have to do it.

To do this, coordinate the lower and upper wing termination points for the flying wires. This can only be done with the wings set up in their correct locations. Most 1/32 scale kits have the flying wire locations marked or have holes in the wings and fuselage. Even so, it's a good idea to check your documentation.

If you have no documentation you can still install flying wires following these general guidelines: The flying wires on the struts from the fuselage to the upper wing are usually crisscrossed. The flying wires are always crisscrossed parallel to the fuselage, and sometimes perpendicular to it. Normally, two sets of flying wires connect the upper and lower wings on both sides of the fuselage, and two wires make up each set. One set usually runs from the forward part on the lower wing near the fuselage and terminates at the outer section of the forward end of the upper wing. The second set starts from the forward end of the outboard area of the lower wing and terminates at the mid-section or outboard end of the upper wing close to the fuselage. These two sets of wires can't be located along the same line or they will be bent around one another, so be careful how you locate them. Use dividers to set the distances between pairs of wires.

Some manufacturers set up their models to accept thread as the flying wire rigging; there are tabs where the wires go. A good example of this is

When you are ready to attach struts to the wings, tape the parts together, position the wings and struts, and glue them in place with super glue applied with a thin wire applicator.

Once the struts are glued in place, it's easier to work with the subassemblies and then reassemble the wings.

If the kit has no locations for flying wire, you can add them without much effort. The addition of flying wires on Glenco's Grumman Duck really help make this old kit worth the building time.

Elmer's glue makes excellent filler for wing struts, especially if there are large voids to fill.

Monogram's F3F Grumman Gulfhawk, which has both tabs and holes. The best thing to do in this case is remove the tabs and use the holes for the flying wires. Don't use thread for any applications; it collects dust, which is just about impossible to remove.

When you are ready to assemble the struts and upper wing, first paint the fuselage and lower wing, then glue them together. Paint the struts and upper wing separately and then attach them. Keeping the upper wing and the struts separate will allow a quality paint finish, since airbrushing the underside of the wing and interior struts after they are attached is difficult. This useful technique creates a problem if you are building a triplane,

however. Keeping the mid and upper wings separate until after you paint the fuselage and lower wing assembly means that you will have to do some good fit work on the mid wing—you will not be able to do any filling and sanding after it is attached.

When you are ready to assemble the struts and the upper wing, position all the parts with masking tape. Remove paint from the gluing surfaces of the strut attachment points on the wings and the tips of the struts. When the wings and struts are positioned, apply a drop of super glue to the lower strut locations with thin wire. When the glue dries, turn the model over and do the upper strut locations. Be careful not to let glue

bleed onto the wing surfaces—you only need a small amount at each location. To fill the voids where the struts attach to the wings use Elmer's glue or Kristal Kleer as filler and a toothpick as an applicator. Paint the filler the same color as the wing.

Now you can add flying wires. The best material for flying wires is real wire. Most hobby stores carry three-foot (1m) sections of piano wire. You can also order stainless steel wire from Small Parts Inc. or use thin spool wire. For 1/32 scale kits I recommend gauge 74 to gauge 77; for 1/48 and 1/72 scale, gauge 77 to gauge 79. Piano wire or the stainless wire is ideal for all scales because it is stiff and will not sag. For 1/48 scale and smaller, use spool wire if the lengths of the flying wires are no more than 3 or 4 inches (76.2 to 101.6 mm). Spool wire is easy to straighten, but it is not stiff, and lengths of more than four inches tend to sag. If you use it, simply stretch a length by holding the ends with pliers and pulling in opposite directions. You will see the wire straighten and feel it stretch slightly.

Use dividers to measure the distance between the end points of the flying wire. Be sure to add approximately ⅛ inch (3.2 mm) so you will never cut the initial length too short. Next, form-fit the wire into its location. If it is too big, cut a small length off the end of the wire, test fit it, and cut again. I usually get the correct fit on the third or fourth try. The wire should be straight, so check your work. If you are not careful you can get a slight bow that may not become apparent until you install the other wires. Test-fitting flying wires is tedious, and as you add wires it gets even more so because you have to work around those already installed.

I recommend installing wires as you cut them to their proper length. In most instances, once you cut a wire to its correct length and install it, it will not fall out if you have a tight fit. If you are working with pairs of wires, installing both before you glue them

Use a pair of dividers to measure the approximate length of flying wires.

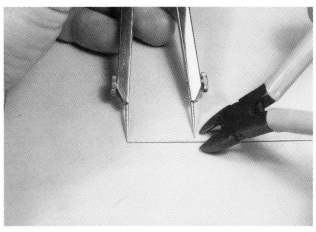

Once you know the correct length, measure a piece of wire, add about 1/8 inch (3.175mm) just to be sure, then cut.

keeps you from mixing up the corresponding holes—which is easy to do if the wires are close to one another. Use Elmer's white glue on all wires.

A final note: If you are using piano wire you will need to sand it to remove surface rust and then paint it. Don't use water-base paints on wire because the paint's carrier, water, will cause the wire to oxidize and discolor. Stainless steel wire does not need to be painted because it does not rust.

CONTROL CABLES

Control cables were exposed on many biplanes, but as aircraft designs improved, aileron and elevator control cables were incorporated into the wings and fuselage. As with flying wires, sometimes kit manufacturers locate holes where control cables emerge and sometimes they don't. Revell did an excellent job providing these holes on their 1/28 scale biplane kits and in supplying control horns (external appendages on a control surface that the cables attach to) for the control surfaces. The old 1/48 scale Aurora kits, which Monogram has recently reissued, had control horns on the control surfaces but no locations for control cables on the

Sometimes you have to bend the end of a wire to get it to sit correctly in its location; otherwise the wire may have a slight bow in it.

Set each wire in place and let the glue dry before doing the next one. This means a long assembly process, but doing it ensures that you won't knock a wire out of position before it has a chance to dry.

Hasegawa's 1/32 scale Peashooter has pre-drilled holes for flying wires. Because of the unusual wire configuration, this model makes an excellent display piece.

fuselage or wings. Matchbox supplied control horns for the tail surfaces on its 1/32 scale Tigermoth, but no hole locations on the fuselage.

If there are no holes in the fuselage for the tail surface control cables, mark them by checking your documentation and drill them into the fuselage. After you start the hole, angle it in the direction of its attachment on the rudder or the elevator. This way the cable will appear angled correctly as it emerges from the fuselage. Be sure the holes on both sides of the fuselage are symmetric.

For control cable material I use stretched clear sprue because it responds well to heat. The exact thickness you need depends on how successful you are at stretching the plastic, so use your best judgment. If the thickness looks good, use it. When I am ready to install the stretched sprue, I thread the wire through the holes in the fuselage and pull it so there are equal lengths on both sides. Glue one side of the stretched sprue to the corresponding control horn using a drop of Elmer's glue. After it dries, pull the other end tight and glue. If you are building a 1/32 scale kit, notch the tops of the control horns so the stretched sprue will ride in the notch. This makes it easy to hold the sprue taut, since you can pull it past the control horn and tape it to your workbench.

On smaller scale models you will have to glue the sprue as best you can and use the blown-out match trick to get it taut. Light a wooden match, blow it out, and quickly position the tip about ½ inch (12.7 mm) below the sprue. The hot smoke from the match

(Left, center) When attaching control cables, you can use masking tape to hold them while the glue dries.

(Bottom) Once the glue dries, cut the sprue and apply a small drop of Elmer's to hide the cut tip. After the glue is dry, paint it to blend in with the control horn.

If you have a problem positioning the control cable on top of the control horn, notch the tip so the sprue will ride in the notch.

will cause the plastic to tighten. Be careful not to melt or distort the plastic, which is easy to do if you get too close with the match.

If the model has no control horns you can make them from plastic stock, but be sure to locate them on both sides of the rudder and ailerons at the same locations. The edges and the tops of control horns should be tapered; on 1/48 scale and 1/72 scale you can use small plastic rod to simulate them. Remember that control cables for ailerons emerged from the upper and lower surface of the wing. Elevators had four control cables emerging from the fuselage (two per side), and rudders had two cables emerging from the fuselage (one per side). After you have installed all control cables, add a touch of paint to the tops of the control horns so the cable tips and Elmer's glue can't be seen.

ANTENNA WIRES

All propeller-driven aircraft had some type of wire antenna extending from a vertical antenna to the tail. These antennas also served as receivers for radio direction equipment, so even if the aircraft did not have a radio, it may still have had some direction-finding gear. WW I-era planes did not have radios or electronic gear, so don't add any antennas to these models. On the other hand, jet aircraft have no external antenna lines or cables because of the speed of the aircraft.

Make antenna wires from clear sprue, stretched and installed the same way as control cables. You may have to drill a hole into the upper area of the leading edge of the rudder or in the fuselage and wings, as is the

Cable-type antennas are attached just like control cables, except that you are usually not working in confined areas.

The secondary antenna (vertical wire) on this Corsair was positioned by gluing it to the fuselage first, then taping the upper end to an adjustable lamp positioned so the stretched sprue lengths touched. This technique ensured that both the horizontal and vertical antenna wires would be taut.

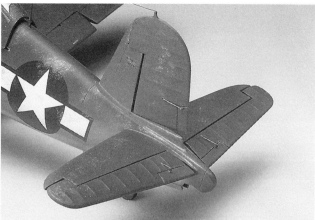

Modern antennas are usually small protrusions or small square or rectangular shapes. The multiple antenna arrays on Testor's 1/72 scale Douglas B-66B, which was converted to an EB-66E, were made from thin sheet stock. (Model by Major Billy Crisler, USAF.)

Another nice touch is to remove the molded-on detail for trim tabs and add the control cables and horns. The tail surface of Revell's 1/32 scale Corsair looks much better with these details added.

case with the B-17 Flying Fortress and the P-40 Warhawk.

Start from one location, apply the Elmer's glue, let it dry, and glue the other end. It is a lot harder to get the sprue taut during gluing, so get it as tight as possible and use the blown-out match trick. This will only work on stretched sprue of small diameter—on thicker lengths the plastic will distort or melt. You have to develop a feel for stretching sprue; I recommend that you practice and keep your successful practice runs for future projects.

On modern jets, antennas usually look like small, thin squares, rectangles, or large bumps on the fuselage. Thin sheets of stock cut to size using square or rectangular templates are all you will need for these. The trick is to attach them straight—this is especially critical if you have a series of them. To create bumps, use scrap stock and shape with sandpaper. Attach both the square or rectangular and bump-type antenna with super glue and paint wherever plastic sprue touches either a vertical antenna or the model.

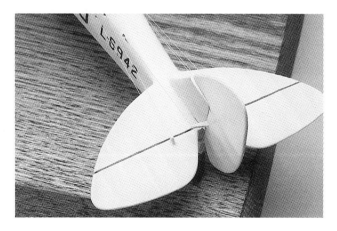

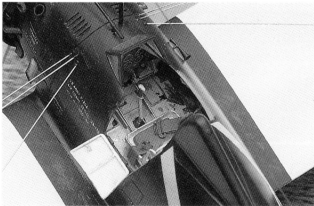

Although Matchbox supplies control horns for its 1/32 scale Tigermoth, you have to drill the holes in the fuselage. The control cables are clear sprue, and they are attached to the control horns with Elmer's white glue.

A detail that modelers sometimes miss is adding the control cables to the rudder pedals and the control stick.

CHAPTER SIX

REMOVING & REATTACHING PARTS

Removing and reattaching control surfaces adds realism to Hasegawa's 1/48 scale Zero.
(Model by Major Billy Crisler, USAF.)

The overall appearance of model aircraft can be greatly enhanced by removing and reattaching control surfaces, flaps, hatches, and access panels. Real aircraft—especially military aircraft—are in constant use and are continually being cleaned, serviced, and repaired. They are seldom found with all control surfaces in the neutral position, flaps retracted, all hatches closed, and access panels attached.

Removing parts, especially the control surfaces, is time-consuming. It takes a lot of finishing work to get them just right. Filling in voids created by cutting out the parts, adding interior detail, replacing hinges, and

fixing spacing problems all take time, but if you follow the techniques presented here and build on them as you gain experience, you will soon find yourself cutting out parts on almost every model you build.

CONTROL SURFACES

The difficulty of removing and reattaching ailerons, rudders, and elevators depends on the scale of the model, how it's constructed, and whether you will cut through or around the hinges. Before you try to remove control surfaces, review documentation to see how much spacing there is between the control surfaces

and wings. Also note their positioning and how much movement they have. Typically, elevators and rudders have pronounced movement on most aircraft, while the design of ailerons varies greatly.

Plan how you are going to remove parts. On most aircraft the spacing between control surfaces and wing attachment locations is small, so remove as little plastic as possible. Control surfaces on large scale aircraft usually require much more work than smaller scale kits, because on large scale kits hinges are large enough to be noticed if they are missing. On kits 1/72 scale and smaller

(Left) Reproducing the hinge detail on Hasegawa's 1/32 scale Peashooter was easy, thanks to Evergreen's selection of various sizes of plastic strips.

(Center) The elevator control surfaces on Monogram's B-25 were cut out with a scriber and thin razor saw. Large hinges are best left alone, while smaller ones can be easily replaced.

they are so small that replacing them may not be necessary.

Start by removing the rudder, then the elevators, and finally the ailerons. Don't remove them all at once, as the amount of work required to refinish all the parts may seem overwhelming. If you mark the control surfaces as you remove them you will know which aileron or elevator goes with what wing. When removing control surfaces, glue the halves together first to ensure that wings, fuselage areas, and control surfaces have the correct contours.

Control surfaces are almost always engraved, which makes them easy to cut out—the channels formed by engraving makes scribing and cutting easy. The tools of choice are a scriber, scribing needle, razor saw, and a jeweler's saw. Before cutting, protect the surrounding plastic with one or two layers of masking tape.

For control surfaces, check the hinges to see if it will be easier to cut through or around them. If they are thin and short and don't protrude into the control surface very far, cut through them. This makes scribing easier because you are not cutting around small details. If you cut through the hinges, use a straightedge as a guide for the first few runs. Once you match the engraving depth you can cut along the entire length.

If the hinges are long, like those on the rudder of a 1/48 scale B-29, you may want to cut around them. If you cut through them and glue on a new hinge, you must treat it carefully, especially if you have to sand, scrape, or file it. A long piece of plastic with a small area for gluing tends to snap off.

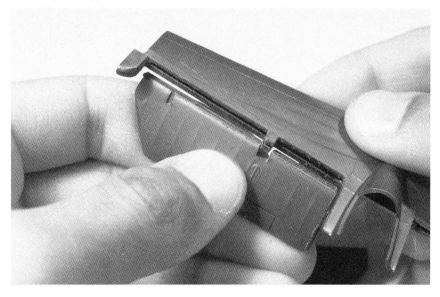

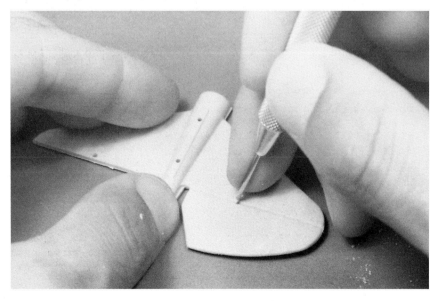

Even a simple scribing needle can remove control surfaces. To achieve clean cuts, be sure the tip is sharp.

Hold the scriber firmly and maintain positive control. It's easy to run past the engraved channel and gouge the surrounding plastic. You may have to vary the angle between the scriber and the surface of the plastic to prevent it from binding. If you are using a scribing needle, make sure it's sharp, hold the tool at approximately 45 degrees to the surface of the plastic, and move it in one direction along the engraved channel. If you are going to cut through hinges, use a scriber. If you're cutting around hinges, stick with a scribing needle. The scribing needle takes longer to cut through plastic and requires more cleanup, but it works better around sharp corners.

During the first few passes, the scribing tool may stop and start until it cuts into the plastic. Run it along channels in one direction. When the channels are deep enough (a matter of judgment) work the corners and deepen them until the tool runs smoothly as it changes direction. As you get closer to cutting through the plastic, it will turn white along the scribing line.

The depth of the scribing line won't be uniform, and the tip may completely cut through sections, causing the scribing tool to bind. When this happens, reduce the pressure and decrease the angle between the tool and the surface. Cut through the plastic on one side only, then turn it over and repeat the process on the opposite side.

While you would probably do this as a matter of course with 1/32 and 1/48 scale kits, there is a temptation to cut all the way through from one side with 1/72 scale kits. Avoid doing so, because the engravings for control surfaces are sometimes not lined up exactly on the upper and lower wings. While this can easily be corrected with strip stock after you complete the cuts, it is difficult if some of the control surface as well as the engraved channel is still attached to one side of the wing area, which is what might happen if you cut all the way through from one side.

Don't try to snap the plastic on control surfaces because the plastic around hinges won't give as easily as a straight line would. Snapping the part may break the hinges. It can also

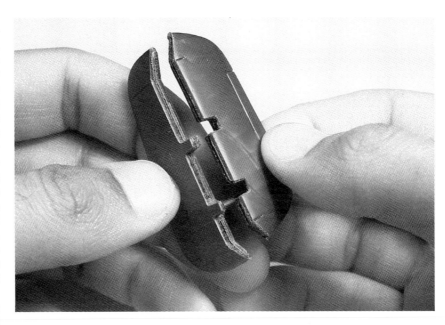

Cutting all the way through the thick rudder as well as around the hinges on this 1/48 scale part wasn't difficult, but it did take some time.

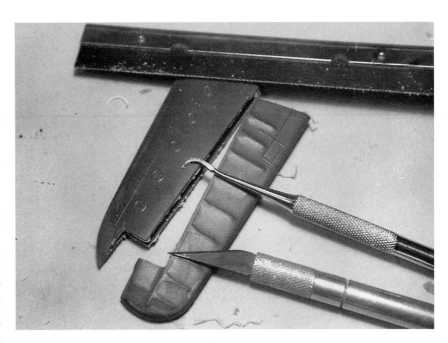

A razor saw cut through the end of this control surface while the scriber did the rest. Once the parts were separated, an X-Acto knife was used to clean the excess plastic from the newly cut edges.

cause edges to be angled, which means additional work when parts don't fit back into their locations.

Razor saws or jeweler's saws can be used for cutting short lengths such as the ends of control surfaces or the sides of control tabs. To ensure that the saw blade does not migrate away from the intended cut line, scribe a

deep channel for it to follow. I have had some bad experiences using a jeweler's saw to cut long lengths, so I recommend confining it to small jobs.

Trim tabs, which are really small control surfaces attached to larger control surfaces, usually need outlines engraved deeper to stand out more. Cut through the sides of trim

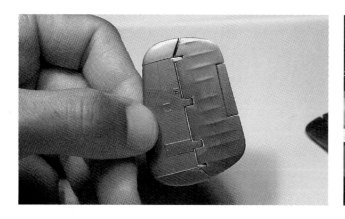

The top and bottom areas of this trim tab were cut with a jeweler's saw. The scribed detail was deepened, so the tab could be bent.

The finished tail surface on this Monogram's 1/48 scale B-25J clearly shows how repositioning control tabs adds another level of realism to a model.

I deepened the control tab engravings on Revell's 1/32 scale Corsair instead of cutting the ends through. With the addition of control horns and cables, the control tabs look like they are ready to move at any moment.

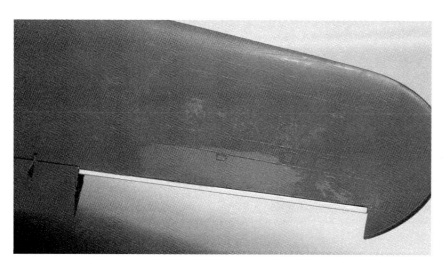

tabs with a razor saw or a jeweler's saw, but don't remove them; the trim tab can be easily bent into a more realistic up/down or left/right position after the engraving along the length of the control tab is deepened. Be sure to deepen the engraving on both sides. Many manufacturers mold control surface cables for the control tabs onto the wing. To add realism, remove the molded-on detail, drill a hole into the wing where the cable emerges, and add a small stub on the control horn made from strip stock. Slip thin electronics wire into the hole in the wing and attach it to the stub with Elmer's glue.

SPACING PROBLEMS WITH CONTROL SURFACES

After cutting out the control surfaces, clean up the cut lines and remove excess plastic. Check the fit between the wing and control surface and especially between hinges and hinge openings. You will find spacing at these locations that must be filled, particularly at hinges. The spaces resulted when plastic was removed by scribing and cutting. If the engraving lines on the upper and lower wing

If the aileron control surface on Monogram's 1/48 scale B-25 had been completely cut through from the top of the wing, a section of the lower control surface would still be attached to the wing and would make repairs difficult. The solution on this wing was easy because the aileron was cut through from both sides.

surfaces were not lined up, add strip stock to even out the opening on one side while removing plastic on the other. I usually add the strip stock to the wing and then run the control surface across sandpaper to even up the edges.

Spacing problems between control surfaces and wings can also be a problem with kits that supply separate control surfaces. Kits such as Revell's 1/32 scale Spitfire and P-40 Warhawk and Matchbox's 1/32 scale Bf 109 have such problems; they can be easily fixed the same way.

Control surfaces should fit snugly. There should be no space between hinges and hinge openings, little spacing along the leading edge of the control surface and the wing, and no space on the ends. In most cases the spacing can be easily filled. Use strip stock if the spacing is along the length of the control surface, and sheeting if it is along a hinge or at the ends of the control panel.

To determine what size plastic strip or sheeting you need, position the control surface and secure it with tape. Start adding pieces of plastic where a space must be filled. Normally you can find strip stock or sheeting close to the size you need. It is always easier to use a larger size and sand it down than to build up the area. It may be necessary to stack several thicknesses to get the correct size, and sometimes you will have to sand it down after you attach it.

Don't try to get all the spacing resolved at once. It's too easy to mix things up. Start by getting the positioning of the control surface correct

Revell's 1/32 scale P-40 is a good kit, but there are spacing problems on the already detached control surfaces. They can easily be fixed with some Evergreen sheet stock and super glue.

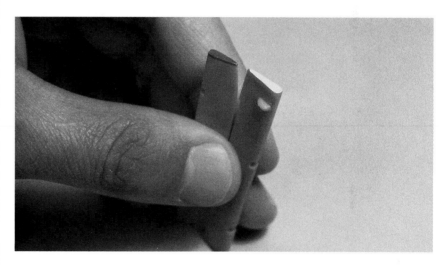

Sheet stock was added to the ends of the ailerons on Monogram's 1/32 scale F3F for a tight fit.

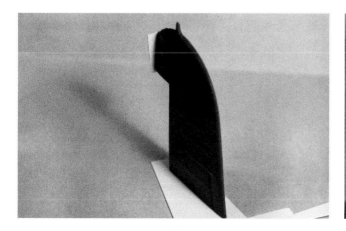

It's easier to work with oversized sheet stock than to try to measure and cut an exact size.

Fixing the spacing problems on small parts with hinges might seem overwhelming at first, but if you take it a step at a time, it's no big deal.

The vertical stabilizer on this Corsair has been completed and silver paint was used to detect cracks or flaws. Super glue will be added to any problem areas and after sanding the paint will be removed with Polly-S paint and decal remover.

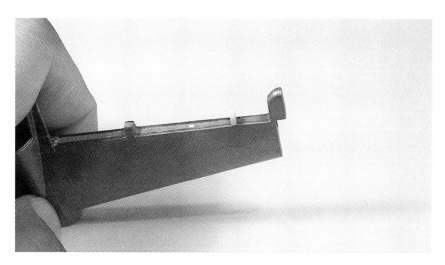

by adding plastic sheeting to the ends. Then you can set the control surface into place without having to tape each time. For a rudder, do the bottom and uppermost hinge contact surface area so it will stay in place.

Once the ends are complete and positioning is correct, add strip stock to the edge of the wing to reduce spacing, then start on hinges or hinge openings. If the openings are uniform it really doesn't matter where you add sheeting. The sheets for the hinges will be small, which makes applying them a tedious process, especially if you must add plastic to the front of the hinge.

In most cases it's easier to glue a piece of oversized sheeting to its location and form-fit it. Attach all sheeting with white tube super glue applied with the thin wire applicator. After the glue dries and you have cut and sanded the plastic sheet to shape, run a bead of glue around the edge. Although you will have to sand again, applying the second coat will ensure that the sheeting is completely blended in with the plastic and that no cracks remain. Attaching the sheeting becomes almost intuitive as you gain experience. You will soon be able to judge a part and determine the best and easiest location for placement of the plastic and be able to control the appearance of hinges and hinge openings. After you have fixed all the spacing problems, apply silver paint to detect flaws. If you find problems, simply add super glue and refinish.

FILLING VOIDS

Whenever you remove a control surface you will have a void in the wing and the control surface that must be filled or covered. Areas where hinges are located should already be covered, but you still need to do something along the length of the opening on the wing and along the control surface. When you remove control surfaces you weaken the wing and the plastic may sag along the center of the area where the part was

If you have to use putty as a filler, place a plastic wedge inside the part. This gives the part extra strength, prevents the surface from flexing, and preserves the shape.

removed. Filling these voids adds strength and prevents sagging. There are several options for filling voids, including using plastic strip stock, plastic sheeting, thick gel super glue, or two-part resin. The type of filler will depend on the scale of the model and the depth and size of the opening.

If you are working with a 1/72 scale kit you can cover the voids on the wing and control surface with small strip stock or thin sheeting. If you use strip stock you will have to form-fit the lengths into place. If you are using sheeting you can cut an approximate length, glue it in place, and cut and sand to the correct shape. Be careful not to ruin the shape of the hinge on the wing or the hinge opening on the control surface. Always use super glue to attach the plastic and fill in any cracks.

To fill in the interior area of the wing or control surface to give the area some extra strength, squeeze thick gel super glue into the void and add accelerator. The quick gel will appear to defy gravity. I have had good success applying it over an opening as large as ⅛ inch (31.8 mm). Use a flat-tipped X-Acto blade to smooth out the glue before adding the accelerator.

If you are working with 1/32 scale kits, fill the control surface voids and tail surfaces with two-part resin. Two-part resin fills voids completely and easily and adds strength. With 1/32 scale parts the seams on control and tail surfaces will crack as you sand, scrape, and shape them because the parts are big and the contact surfaces that hold them together are small. Resin prevents this from happening.

To apply it, be sure the seams are sealed and mask along the edge of the opening, covering the entire surface of the part. This will prevent overflow resin from sticking to the surface. Mask the part between two pieces of balsa wood. Be sure it is level so resin will not flow out one side. The wood will act as the stand while you pour the resin. The plastic will get hot as the resin cures; you can reduce the heat by applying a small ice pack to the sides of the plastic. The resin will not stick to the plastic well, and if you were to break the control surface in two you would have a perfect casting of its interior. If the

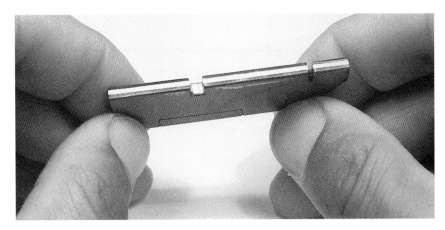

Plastic strip stock makes an excellent filler in areas where there are no protrusions like hinges.

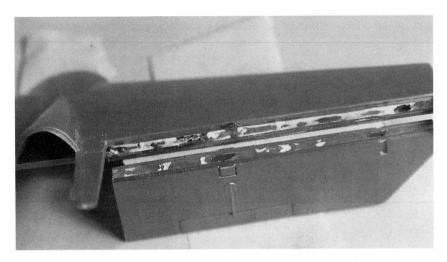

Duro's Quick Gel super glue makes an excellent filler and the glue can be sanded and shaped. The white coloring on the glue is caused by the accelerator.

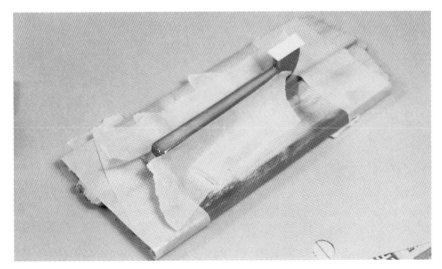

This control surface was filled with two-part casting resin. Masking tape prevents spillover resin from attaching to the plastic. Resin is the best filler because it adds weight and increases strength in hollow parts, especially on 1/24 and 1/32 scale kits.

(Left) The resin on this part has been sanded and shaped by running it across a stationary piece of sandpaper. To protect the surface detail on the part, cover it with masking tape.

(Center) Oversized sheet stock can be trimmed down to its approximate size with a #11 X-Acto blade and then sanded and shaped.

opening is large I sometimes insert a piece of strip stock in the center of the void and glue it in place. After the glue has dried I pour the resin into the void. The strip stock prevents the hardened resin from moving or separating from the interior surface.

Once the resin has dried you can sand and shape it any way you want. You can use resin in combination with both strip stock and sheeting. Reserve the plastic for covering small areas, but use thick enough stock to sand and shape it.

For wing openings, form-fit sections of sheet stock into place and glue them. Once the glue is dry, sand and shape the sheeting so it's flush with the wing. If the wing flexes and you want to add strength, pile some quick gel super glue inside until it touches both inner surfaces and add accelerator. Another method is to insert some wedges into the interior of the wing and glue them into place. As you fill in the voids, check your work frequently by fitting the control surface into its location.

As a final step, round off the leading edges so they are contoured correctly by running them along sandpaper while you rotate the part. A few passes on both sides will do it.

REPLACING HINGES

Even if you can cut around the engraved hinges of control surfaces you may still find yourself replacing them. Sometimes no matter how careful you are when cutting, hinges get ruined or snap off.

When you are ready to start

As you add sheet stock, check the fit on the wing and control surface. Be sure to duplicate the placement and positioning of sheet stock on elevators and ailerons so the parts will match.

On a Corsair the elevators have rounded leading edges and the tail surface has an indented semicircular shape. To duplicate these surface arrangements, run the tail across a dowel covered with sandpaper.

replacing hinges, position the control surface and select the plastic stock that most closely approximates the hinge opening size. Don't try to shape the size of the plastic stock until after you attach it. Start with a slightly larger size and sand it down. This is a repetitive process; it is important to do hinges one at a time to ensure a proper fit. Sometimes the plastic stock is an almost-perfect fit. In these cases, remove the necessary plastic and slide the stock into the hinge opening to check the fit.

Carefully apply a small drop of white tube super glue where the hinges contact the wing surface. Remove the control surface after the glue dries. Next run a bead of super glue along the perimeter of each hinge.

When all the hinges associated with a control surface are in place, be sure they line up and cut them to

The completed tail surface on Revell's 1/32 scale Corsair has all resin filled parts. The control surfaces fit snugly against their wing surfaces—thanks to careful sanding and form-fitting.

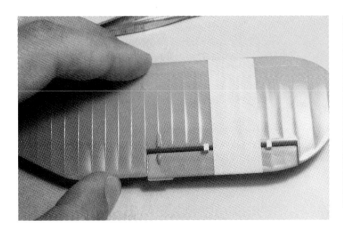 

Micro files were used to cut and shape the hinge locations on this F3F aileron. The size of the opening on the aileron matches the strip stock size that will be used as a hinge.

Always run a bead of super glue around the edge of each piece of strip stock before you cut and shape for maximum strength, and fill all cracks or voids. Once again, protect all surfaces before you start cutting.

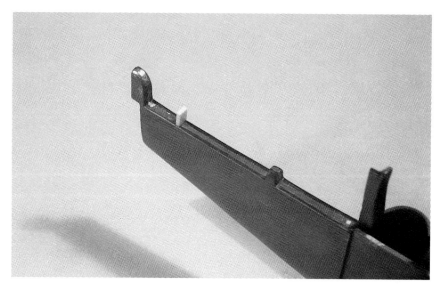

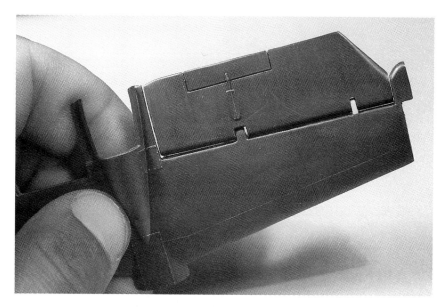

their proper lengths by masking the surrounding wing surface and cutting the plastic that protrudes above with a razor saw. If the plastic strip is small, position the wing or fuselage onto a small hard block of wood so the hinge will be in contact with the wood base. This is where these small hardwood sanding blocks come in handy. Cut the excess plastic with a #11 X-Acto blade by placing the knife blade on the backside of the plastic and cutting toward the wood block. This will keep you from putting stress on the glue joint. After you have finished cutting, apply a drop of super glue where the hinge contacts the wing to seal it and provide a good surface for sanding and shaping.

When you are ready to shape the hinges, mask the wing area to protect surrounding surface detail. Sand the hinges flush with the wing using a small sanding block wrapped in sandpaper. To ensure that no seams remain between the hinge and the attachment area, apply silver paint. If you find flaws, apply more super glue and sand smooth.

Hinges have round edges, and this shape is easy to achieve with a sanding block. The trick is to give all the hinges the same contoured appearance.

It does not take much contact between the sandpaper and the plastic to round off edges, so go slowly and check your work as you progress. Sanding with a rotating motion, it usually takes no more than two or three strokes to round off the edge. When you are finished, run an X-Acto blade along the edges to remove any residual plastic.

Always check for flaws as a last step prior to painting. Silver paint or gray primer can be used as a flaw detector, but be sure to remove it before the final painting.

Edges on hinges can be rounded with sandpaper wrapped around a small sanding block. Rotate the sanding block as you move it across the hinge.

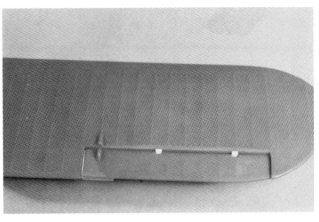

The aileron on Monogram's 1/32 scale F3F is finally ready for painting. Note that sheet plastic has been added to both sides of the aileron and the rounded edges of the hinges are no higher than the aileron's surface.

The aileron on this F3F looks as though it is about to move thanks to some extra plastic and a little elbow grease. Note the added control cable. These small details greatly enhance realism.

FLAPS

There is a fundamental difference between removing control surfaces and removing flaps. Control surfaces are removed after the wing halves are glued together, while flaps can be removed either before or after the halves are glued. In either case, use the same techniques for removing flaps as you used for removing control surfaces. On large aircraft, such

The repositioned flaps and slats on Monogram's 1/48 scale Prowler makes a world of difference in the kit's appearance. Adding these types of details is what modeling is all about-- taking a good kit and making it better. (Model by Scott Weller.)

If the flap has an engraved channel, the easiest way to cut through the plastic is to use a scriber.

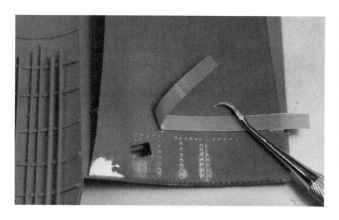

If the flap has no engraved channel, like the upper flap detail on Revell's Corsair, use labeling tape to guide the scriber.

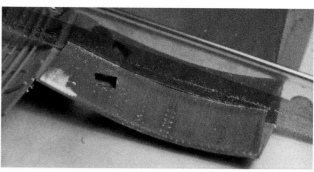

Sometimes you can get away with using a razor saw to speed up your work, but it is important to have a cutting guide. In this case the scriber cut a channel and the job was finished with the saw.

as two-and four-engine bombers, flaps are usually on the lower wing. On propeller-driven fighters flaps can be either on the lower wing or a part of the entire trailing edge, so that when they are actuated, that section of the wing actually moves. On jets you can have both flaps and slats. (Slats is another name for the flaps that extend from the leading edge of the wing.)

When you cut out flaps you will probably use a combination of scribers, a razor saw, and an X-Acto knife. The surface detail will usually be recessed, so use a scriber to get a deep channel before using a razor saw to finish. When a saw won't work, take your time and use the scriber. On some kits the flaps are outlined with raised detail. In these instances,

use labeling tape as a guide and cut along the raised line with a scriber.

Once the parts are removed, clean off excess plastic on the wings and the flaps and sand the edges flat. If the flap is the trailing edge of the wing and it simply rotates downward, simply close the void in the wing with strip stock where you cut out the flap. If it rotates downward and outward you may need to add interior detailing such as framing, but this depends on how far you extend it.

Flaps also need the addition of plastic stock. The sides need sheet stock and the front will need thicker strip stock, which should be sanded and shaped. If you extend the flaps far enough, you will expose the flap's rod actuators, which can be easily duplicated with plastic rod.

If the flaps are part of the lower wing, you may have to add interior framing using the same techniques as framing the inside of a cockpit. Framing can be duplicated with plastic strips placed at equal intervals along the length of the underside of the flap and the inside of the wing. The size of the strips should appear to be in scale. When you are ready to add framing, cut the number you will need and add about an inch to each strip to make them easy to position. After the strips are applied, cut them flush with the edges and contour the trailing edges of the framing by running the edge of a sanding block across each frame edge.

If you don't have photographs of interior detailing at the flap locations, take a guess. At a minimum you will

The repositioned flaps on Revell's 1/32 scale Corsair look a lot better than the kit's engraved flap detail. Note the actuator rod between the two outer flaps.

Adding detail to the interior of the wing can be as simple as adding a piece of sheet plastic. Adding interior framing in areas of the wing exposed by an extended flap would be a more complicated endeavor.

Removing the flaps on a Corsair is one of the more difficult flap repositioning projects because the flaps are curved. The leading edges of all flaps need additional plastic.

The completed right side flaps for a Corsair. To get them to fit correctly, sheet stock was also added to the sides.

Always check your work, especially on complicated flap or slat arrangements.

find rows of framing on both the inside area of the flaps and the interior of the wing. When you have added the framing, paint the inside areas. Finally, add a faint dusting of black pastel with a flat brush to dirty up the interior.

REMOVING & DETAILING HATCHES & ACCESS PANELS

If you are cutting out access panels or hatches and the parts are engraved, use the same techniques as you used for control surfaces. If the parts have raised plastic outlines as many models have, scribe them out using labeling tape as a guide. Use a needle scriber on the initial channel; its thin sharp tip will more easily follow the outline defined by the tiny plastic ridge. Don't use a lot of pressure—let the tip guide itself along the ridge and run it along the ridge side closest to the part to be cut out. This is a matter of feel, so go slowly and stop frequently to rest your hand. Once you have a shallow channel you can add more pressure or switch to a scriber that removes plastic.

Now clean up the edges of the hatches and the locations they were cut from. Carefully sand the surfaces after masking surrounding areas to protect detail, especially hinge detail along the edge of a hatch.

Access panels are usually much thinner than hatches, as they are usually part of the aircraft's outer skin. Thin the parts the way you thin land-

The simple flap rotation on a P-51 Mustang makes it an ideal kit for trying your hand at cutting out flaps. This Monogram kit looks a lot better with repositioned flaps. (Model by Richard Boutin, Sr.)

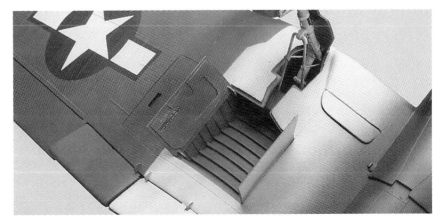

Sometimes flaps had external hinges. Check your documentation.

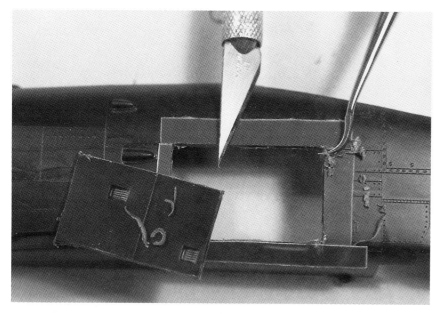

ing gear bay doors. Select a curved or rounded surface with the same contour as the part, wrap sandpaper around it, and run the part across the sandpaper.

Wooden dowels will provide the approximate diameters you need to thin parts. If they are not the right size, try paint bottles or other containers. Use rough-grade paper to get the plastic to the thickness you want and higher grades to smooth it out. Since it doesn't take long to thin plastic, check your progress often. Rotate the part every few strokes for even thinning. If the part is flat, run it across stationary sandpaper. Reverse every few strokes or sand with a figure eight motion.

If your documentation shows backside framing or plating, adding it will enhance the part's appearance. Framing is easy to install, as long as you are using plastic strips of the correct thickness cut to their proper lengths. Use the same techniques as framing cockpits and landing gear.

(Left) A Verlinden detail set was used to detail the exposed electronics bays on Monogram's 1/48 scale A-10. New doors were also supplied by Verlinden, but the kit's cut out parts were used instead. (Model by Scott Weller.)

Needle scribers work best for cutting out small hatches that have rounded corners.

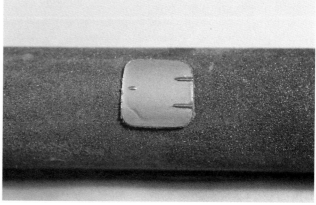

Curved cut-out parts need to be thinned on a curved surface. For large scale parts you can usually find a jar or plastic container with the correct diameter.

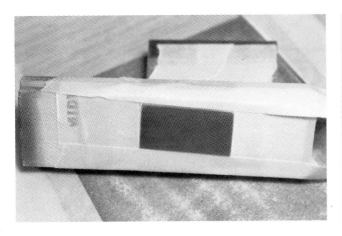

Flat surfaces can be thinned by taping them to balsa wood and running the part across stationary sandpaper. If you choose to use your hands, stand by to lose some skin on your fingertips!

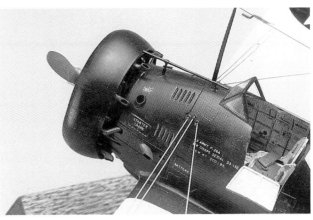

The access hatch on this 1/32 scale Peashooter by Hasegawa was repositioned, and framing was also added to the inside of the hatch.

To trace a curved part onto sheet stock, use the same dowel or container size that you used for thinning the part.

If the part has no noticeable framing on the backside but has an inner surface similar to the insides of some landing gear doors, reproduce it in the same way. Trace a new part on sheet stock using the cut-out part as a guide, and add hole locations, if any. Cut out the new part, punch out the holes using Waldron's punch tool, and glue it to the kit's part using super glue and a thin wire applicator.

If the hatch you are removing has a window, modify the clear plastic part by cutting off the positioning tabs and filling in the corresponding

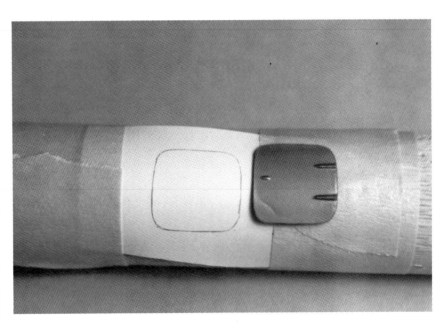

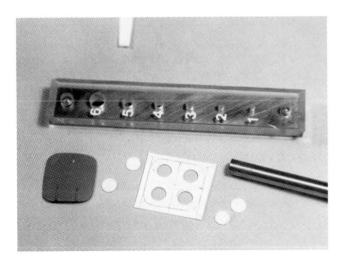

Waldron's punch tool has hundreds of uses and makes cutting out holes a snap.

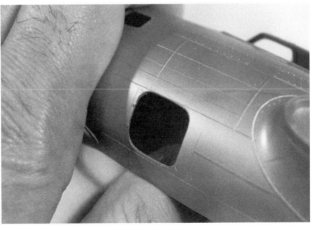

After you cut out access panels or hatches, don't forget to thin the area the part was cut from. Otherwise the hatch opening will look strange.

Aside from removing hatches and access panels, don't forget that naval aircraft look good with folded wings. Every collection of aircraft should have at least one. (Model by Major Billy Crisler, USAF.)

Although this Hasegawa 1/48 scale Corsair II already has open access panels, attention to painting details can make or break the appearance of a model. (Model by Major Billy Crisler, USAF.)

holes on the back. This requires careful cutting and gluing. Be patient when modifying clear parts, and make sure the plastic will seat properly.

Another detail that must be added is the framing around the opening of the access panel or hatch within the fuselage. This is the framing that the door, hatch, or access panel will seat against when closed. It should protrude from around the part's opening for accuracy. Add this and any other detail to the interior before you glue the halves together, whether they are fuselage or wing halves. In some cases, as in the 1/48 scale bomber series by Monogram, the interior detail is there, and all you have to add is small strips of framing around the opening. There is no trick to this. All the techniques presented in this chapter can be applied to this last step. Just remember that each situation is different and may require variations on the basic techniques.

CONCLUSION

After you have selected the model you want to build, you should also decide what details, modifications, and scratchbuilding you want to add before you begin to build. If you were to try all the techniques and projects presented in this book at one time, it would overwhelm you. Pick two or three of the techniques that intrigue you most, then continually add to your list of accomplishments as you build more models. I also encourage you to improve and modify my techniques. There is often a different or better way to achieve the same results. Aside from the fun of trying something new, it will stretch the bounds of your creativity and your imagination.

It is also important to keep in mind that you are going to have a few disasters along the way. Even when your modeling skills are advanced, you will still have disasters. Any modeler who says he or she does not is either lying or does not truly build models. So take a break if you get to the point where you have that wild urge to test-fly your model across the free space of your workroom. It's only a hobby, and it is supposed to be relaxing, not raising your blood pressure! Happy modeling—and please do not forget the kid on the bike who yearns to be creative and imaginative.

MANUFACTURERS AND SUPPLIERS

Badger Airbrush
9128 West Belmont Ave.
Franklin Park, IL 60131
(Airbrush Equipment)

Bare Metal Foil Company
P. O. Box 82
Farmington, MI 48332
(Plastic polish and plastic scriber)

Borden Inc.
Department CP
Columbus, OH 43215
(White glue)

Creations Unlimited Hobby Products
2939 Montreat Dr. N.E.
Grand Rapids, MI 49509
(Flex-I-File and sanding sticks)

Devcon Corporation
Danvers, MA 01923
(Two-part epoxy)

Dremel
4915 21st St.
Racine, WI 53401-9989
(Drill bits, cutters, drill press and drill press vise)

Evergreen Scale Models
12808 N.E. 125th Way
Kirkland, WA 98034
(Plastic strips and sheeting)

Floquil-Polly S Color Corporation
4715 State Hwy. 30
Amsterdam, NY 12010-9204

(Paints, plastic prep and paint/decal remover)

K & S Engineering Co.
6917 59th St.
Chicago, IL 60638
(Sandpaper)

Loctite Corporation
Cleveland, OH 44128
(Super glue)

Micro Mark
340 Snyder Ave.
Berkeley Heights, NJ 07922-1595
(Hobby Supplier)

Microscale Industries, Inc.
1570 Sunland Lane
Costa Mesa, CA 92626
(Decal setting solution)

Model Technologies
13472 Fifth St., Suite 12
Chino, CA 91710
(Photoetched parts)

Pacer Technology
9420 Santa Anita Ave.
Rancho Cucamonga, CA 91730
(Super glue accelerator)

Scotch 3M Painters Masking Tape
Box 33053
St. Paul, MN 55133
(Masking tape)

Small Parts Inc.
13980 N.W. 58th Ct.
P. O. Box 4650
Miami Lakes, FL 33014
(Steel wire and hollow wire)

Squadron Shop
1115 Crowley Dr.
Carrollton, TX 75011
(Putty)

Super Scale International, Inc.
2211 Mouton Dr.
Carson City, NV 89706-0471
(Decals, decal setting solutions, and white glue)

Testors Corporation
620 Buckbee St.
Rockford, IL 61104-4891
(Paints, putty, sandpaper, and glue)

Verlinden Productions
Lone Star Industrial Park
811 Lone Star Dr.
O'Fallon, MO 63366
(Model accessories)

Waldron Model Products
P. O. Box 431
Merlin, OR 97532
(Waldron punch set, placards, instruments, and photoetched parts)

X-Acto, Division of Hunt Mfg. Co.
230 S. Broad St.
Philadelphia, PA 19102
(Blades and cutting tools)

INDEX